A CENTURY OF STYLE

A CENTURY OF STYLE

Sandra Barwick

London
GEORGE ALLEN & UNWIN
Boston   Sydney

George Allen & Unwin (Publishers) Ltd,
40 Museum Street, London WC1A 1LU, UK

George Allen & Unwin (Publishers) Ltd,
Park Lane, Hemel Hempstead, Herts HP2 4TE, UK

Allen & Unwin Inc.,
9 Winchester Terrace, Winchester, Mass 01890, USA

George Allen & Unwin Australia Pty Ltd,
8 Napier Street, North Sydney, NSW 2060, Australia

First published in 1984

British Library Cataloguing in Publication Data

Barwick, Sandra
  A Century of Style
1. Costume – Great Britain – History – 19th century
2. Costume – Great Britain – History – 20th century
I. Title
391'.2'0942   GT738
ISBN 0–04–391009–2

Set in 11 on 13 point Palatino by Bedford Typesetters Ltd
and printed in Great Britain
by Richard Clay (The Chaucer Press) Ltd, Bungay, Suffolk

Contents

List of Illustrations   *page* ix
Acknowledgements   xii

Introduction   1

1   Beautiful and Good   4
2   Professional Beauties   27
3   Dress for Dress's Sake   48
4   Beautiful and Wise   71
5   Bohemia, True and Blue   95
6   Beautiful and Bizarre   120
7   The New Lady   135
8   The Princess and the Punk   158

Bibliography   181
Index   185

List of Illustrations

1 & 2.	Two Princesses of Wales (Mansell Collection/Keystone Press)	*page* 6 & 7
3.	Elaborate and conservative evening dress (Mansell Collection)	12
4.	Alexandra in fancy dress (Mansell Collection)	20
5.	A typical carte-de-visite of the Princess of Wales, 1863 (Mansell Collection)	21
6.	The Duchess of Manchester (Mansell Collection)	23
7.	The Countess of Dudley (Mansell Collection)	28
8.	A carefully arranged studio photograph (Raymond Mander & Joe Mitchenson Theatre Collection)	33
9.	Mrs Wheeler (Mansell Collection)	34
10.	Lillie Langtry with Millais (Victoria & Albert Museum: Crown Copyright)	37
11.	The Regimental Ball of the HAC, 1882 (Mansell Collection)	39
12 & 13.	Lillie Langtry (Raymond Mander & Joe Mitchenson Theatre Collection)	40 & 41
14.	One of Lillie's bills from Worth (Raymond Mander & Joe Mitchenson Theatre Collection)	42
15.	Camille Clifford in 1907 (Raymond Mander & Joe Mitchenson Theatre Collection)	46
16.	Ellen Terry in the Whistlerian style (Raymond Mander & Joe Mitchenson Theatre Collection)	50
17.	Ellen Terry in 1881 (Raymond Mander & Joe Mitchenson Theatre Collection)	50
18.	Mrs Cimabue Brown (Mansell Collection)	51
19.	Sarah Bernhardt in *L'Etrangère* (Raymond Mander & Joe Mitchenson Theatre Collection)	53
20.	The Olivia cap (Mansell Collection)	57
21 & 22.	Two artistic families (National Portrait Gallery)	61
23.	Sarah Bernhardt's version of the pierrot suit (Mansell Collection)	62
24.	Bernhardt in 1895 (Mansell Collection)	64
25.	Bernhardt in 1898 (Raymond Mander & Joe Mitchenson Theatre Collection)	66
26.	Mary Anderson (Mansell Collection)	68
27.	The Marchioness of Ripon (Victoria & Albert Museum: Crown Copyright)	73
28.	The Soulful look (National Portrait Gallery)	74

29.	Millicent, Duchess of Sutherland (BBC Hulton Picture Library)	*page* 75
30.	Mrs Harry Cust (National Portrait Gallery)	77
31.	Violet, Marchioness of Granby (National Portrait Gallery)	77
32.	Lady Randolph Churchill (Camera Press)	81
33.	Daisy, Countess of Warwick (BBC Hulton Picture Library)	81
34.	Mrs Patrick Campbell (Mansell Collection)	83
35.	Consuelo, Duchess of Marlborough (National Portrait Gallery)	85
36.	Mary Curzon (National Portrait Gallery)	90
37.	A jewelled icon (Mansell Collection)	91
38.	Mary Curzon's peacock dress (Mary Evans Picture Library)	93
39.	True Bohemia (National Portrait Gallery)	96
40.	Ida Nettleship (National Portrait Gallery: by kind permission of Sir Caspar John)	97
41.	Blue Bohemia (National Portrait Gallery)	99
42.	The Bohemian revival, 1971 (BBC Hulton Picture Library)	99
43.	Pastoral Bohemia (Mansell Collection)	104
44.	Bohemia in American *Vogue* (*Vogue*)	105
45.	Isadora Duncan (Raymond Mander & Joe Mitchenson Theatre Collection)	106
46.	Queen Mary and Suzanne Lenglen (National Portrait Gallery)	109
47.	Mrs Vernon Castle (Private Collection)	111
48.	Lady Diana Manners (BBC Hulton Picture Library)	115
49.	Nancy Cunard (Cecil Beaton photograph: courtesy of Sotheby's Belgravia)	117
50.	*The Green Hat* (Raymond Mander & Joe Mitchenson Theatre Collection)	117
51.	Dorelia John in old age (National Portrait Gallery: by kind permission of Sir Caspar John)	118
52.	Princess Margaret (BIPS)	119
53.	Noel Coward's skit on the Sitwells (Raymond Mander & Joe Mitchenson Theatre Collection)	123
54.	Edith Sitwell in 1956 (BBC Hulton Picture Library)	123
55.	Margot Asquith (Mansell Collection)	125
56.	Edith Sitwell being filmed (Fox Photos)	128
57.	Edith Sitwell in normal dress (Fox Photos)	129
58.	Lady Ottoline Morrell by Cecil Beaton (Cecil Beaton photograph: courtesy of Sotheby's Belgravia)	130
59.	Lady Ottoline in 1912 (National Portrait Gallery)	132
60.	Lady Diana Cooper (BBC Hulton Picture Library)	136
61.	Lady Furness (Keystone Press Agency)	137
62 & 63.	Princess Marina (Keystone Press Agency/Associated Press)	140
64 & 65.	Margaret Whigham (*Illustrated London News*/Topical)	143 & 144
66.	Daisy Fellowes (Cecil Beaton photograph: courtesy of Sotheby's Belgravia)	147

67.   Gertrude Lawrence (Raymond Mander & Joe Mitchenson
       Theatre Collection)   *page* 149
68.   Mrs Simpson in 1937 (Keystone Press Agency)   153
69.   The Duchess of Windsor in 1953 (Central Press)   153
70.   Vivien Leigh (Keystone Press Agency)   157
71 & 72. The two sides of every fashion model (Clive Arrowsmith:
       Sunday Times)   159
73.   Jerry Hall (Camera Press)   161
74.   Jackie Kennedy (BBC Hulton Picture Library)   163
75.   Bianca Jagger (BBC Hulton Picture Library)   166
76.   Jordan   167
77.   Julia   170
78.   Germaine Greer (Camera Press)   173
79.   Dame Freya Stark (Camera Press)   174
80.   The Princess of Wales in her wedding dress (Keystone
       Press Agency)   177

Acknowledgements

Of the many people who have offered help and encouragement with this book I am particularly grateful to Mr Hardy Amies, Margaret, Duchess of Argyll, Lady Alexandra Metcalfe, Sir Sacheverell Sitwell, Miss P. Byrde at the Bath Museum of Costume, Miss S. Beddoe at the Brighton Museum, Miss K. Staniland at the Museum of London, Mr T. Pepper and Mr D. Chandler at the National Portrait Gallery, and Mrs Thomas at the Ellen Terry Museum at Smallhythe, who all gave freely of their time and knowledge. More general thanks are due to Miss Prudence Glynn for two years of entertaining education in the subject of fashion.

Introduction

Many books have been written about fashion designers, about shifts in shape and line and about the influence of social change on dress. The woman inside the clothes has been surprisingly neglected, yet without her the cut of fashion makes little sense. The chapters which follow are about her: more precisely, they are about the style and creativity of some of the women who were well-known for their dress, from the marriage of Princess Alexandra to the Prince of Wales in 1863 to the time of the marriage of the present Princess of Wales.

Women are not just puppets of the mode. They reflect in their dress their background and their social standing, but they also influence each other and if they are well-known they may also have an impact on the readers of magazines and on designers. All, including the most bizarre, reveal something about their period. To make these influences and developments clearer, the chapters have been placed in roughly chronological order. Each contains examples of women who represent influential or important types of the time, women who directed their dress to their own style and ambitions. Many of them have fashion descendants who can be identified today.

I have not included women who were designers, like Chanel or Lucile, or much about those whose appearance was mainly dictated by others in artificial circumstances, like the great film stars of the 1930s or the models of the 1950s and 1960s. Nor is there enough space to mention more than a few of those who deserve a recognition of their creativity, because this is not a comprehensive survey but an attempt to indicate a distinctly feminine contribution to the history of fashion.

Most leaders of fashion possess style in some degree, but what it is is harder to define. Even Lady Diana Cooper, who has been famous for it during much of this century, says she does not know what the word means. It is easier seen than said: some women can take the shabbiest jumble-sale tweed coat, the most vulgar chandelier earrings or a pair of non-matching luminous pink socks and wear them with grace. Others remain irretrievably lumpish in the most elegant and expensive rags.

You may, as Sir Cecil Beaton pointed out, lead a woman to Dior, but you can't make her look good in it.

What it is that makes such a woman look good, or makes other people believe that she does, is easier – and certainly more cheering – to approach through a string of negatives. It is not necessary to be young – Mrs Simpson was in her thirties when she began to be noted as a fashion leader. Because stylists are admired for much more than loveliness of face they can, like the Duchess of Manchester in the last century, remain acknowledged leaders of fashion when their own daughters are adult, and the stylishness of Dorelia John and of Jane Morris remained with them in old age. It is not necessary to be rich – Ellen Terry was struggling against debts when she became a fashion leader in the mid-1870s. It is not, most encouraging of all, necessary to be beautiful. A surprising number of recognised leaders of fashion are decidedly plain and some of them border on ugliness. It is even possible, as Mrs Haweis, fashion journalist and innovator, was reassuring her readership as early as 1878, to turn defects and deformities to good account: 'Do not some people,' she wrote in *The Art of Beauty*, 'admire a cast in the eye, a slight goitre, even a limp? There is a "beauté du diable", stricken with imperfection, but with its own charm.'

But because the appeal of mistresses of fashion is based on more than dress and face – on carriage, on charm, on status and sparkle, on all manner of attributes of personality and tricks of behaviour which are not captured by the camera – it is not easy to identify after the women in question have died. What evidence there is was often tampered with: photographs were retouched (few of the legendary 'natural' beauties of the past were as free from spot and wrinkle as photographs suggest), portraits were flattering, and even the memoirs of the mistress of fashion, though they are often stuffed with descriptions of dresses in lieu of more scandalous disclosures of her affairs, were frequently inaccurate because they were ghosted by someone else. It is as difficult to give a true impression of how Ellen Terry looked as how Oscar Wilde talked: the art of dressing is as ephemeral as the art of conversation.

In view of all this, it is perhaps not surprising that students of fashion devote most of their time to fashion plates and to clothes themselves, which are more tangible than this business of matching skirt to sash, and suiting the tilt of the hat to the head. But if the study of the interaction and influence of women on fashion is a complex and delicate business it has its rewards in its richness of human interest and unexpected detail. 'Black satin,' reported the *World,* a popular Society magazine of the time, on 10 February 1892, 'went violently out of fashion when the notorious Maria Manning elected to be hanged in it.'

Few designers could be as dramatically influential as that.

1
Beautiful and Good

'I have heard,' said the Empress Eugénie to Frederick Ponsonby, 'that your fiancée is beautiful. This is much more important than being good. The world is chockful of good women, but very few are beautiful.'

This epigram was coined at the fin de siècle, but it summarises the philosophy of the fashion empress of the mid-nineteenth century. In the 1860s Eugénie ruled the fashion columns; Worth was her prime minister, and her subjects those women with any interest in dress, who waited eagerly for news of the slightest shrinkage in the measurements of the imperial crinoline, the merest shading of a favoured colour.

On the other side of the Channel, shrouded in black from the moment of her husband's death on 14 December 1861, Queen ('I will be good') Victoria held real power in the land, but almost none in the dress shop. Beauty and dress sense did not feature among the virtues she much admired, and her fervent hope for her heir's prospective bride, the Danish Princess Alexandra, was that she would not attempt to ensnare her son with bows and laces: 'Fashionable dressing – anything but that,' she wrote to her daughter, the Princess Royal.

Luckily for her and for a sentimental nation, the new Princess of Wales, secured in St George's Chapel, Windsor, in 1863, turned out to be both beautiful and good. Only eighteen when she landed at Gravesend before her marriage, dressed in grey and violet half-mourning for the Prince Consort, her white bonnet topped with pink roses, she was already admired by those who knew her as much for her charm of character as for her elegance of dress. It was the period of the sweet Dickensian heroine, and Alexandra was fitted to her time. At once innocent and confident, she was the paradigm of the well-dressed gentlewoman, whose lady-like style of dressing can still be seen amongst supportive wives, whether of politicians, big businessmen or princes.

Alexandra's pre-eminence was the result partly of effort and partly of good fortune, for she was the beauty of her family. She had wide,

4

grey-blue eyes, a peachy skin and a long oval face, which she complemented in 1863 by puffing her hair out at the temples and letting it fall
back on her shoulders in ringlets. Early photographs reveal a slight
chubbiness of face which soon fined down as a result of the hectic social
life she danced through, led by the Prince of Wales, but her figure was
always slim – 'flat as a board' was Queen Victoria's ungracious
comment. Her Coronation dress, worn in 1902 when she was fifty-
seven, reveals that even then she kept a 23-inch waist; amongst her
dumpy Hanoverian in-laws she looked like a greyhound in a pack of
overfed pugs.

Her innocent expression did not vanish with her girlhood, either.
Sarah Bernhardt, typically enthusiastic, noted that it was still evident in
1880, when she met her in Denmark: 'Oh that adorable and seductive
face – with the eyes of a child of the North, and classic features of
virginal purity, a long, supple neck that seemed made for queenly
bows, and a sweet and almost timid smile. The indefinable charm of
this Princess made her so radiant that I saw nothing but her.' It sounds
like sycophancy, but cooler spirits than Sarah's were as extravagant in
their response to Alexandra's looks. Violet Lindsay, a beauty herself,
turned away dancing partners in her girlhood so that she could stand
and watch the Princess's face.

The most characteristic mark of the well-dressed gentlewoman,
though, is not the ability to draw ecstatic praise from those around her,
but a natural instinct for what is suitable in dress. Like the present
Princess of Wales, Alexandra had a fine sense for the conventional
which was responsible for some of her confidence and ease of manner.
Those who watched her could not decide which suited her best – full
evening dress in which, however showy, she could make every other
woman look vulgar, or simple country clothes, in which she made them
look hopelessly overdressed. She even dazzled in 'rough ulster and cap
to drive the miniature four in hand ponies, with silvery bells and dogs
barking round her'.

An instinct for the suitable must come partly from a childhood
absorption of unwritten rules. Nuances of convention are picked up
most swiftly by children of a large family, used to the rules of a group; it
is the only child who commonly stands dismally alone, unsuitably
dressed, on the edge of the Christmas party. Alexandra's family was not
only large but royal. Yet there was much more to her flair in dress than
an abundance of brothers and sisters and good training in manners.
Queen Victoria's eldest child, the Princess Royal, also came from a large

1 & 2 Two Princesses of Wales whose faces the fashion for small, tip-tilted hats particularly became. Above is Diana, before her marriage, in a simple checked dress with a high collar and a flirtatious hat, at Ascot in 1981. On the left, Alexandra looks equally neat and demure in a high-collared jacket and a hat frothing with feathers, photographed by Downey in about 1868. Her trim jacket with its matching skirt is dressmaker, not tailor-made, but there is a hint of a tailored future in its simple lines. Alexandra's face slimmed down from its slight chubbiness soon after her marriage.

family, and she could look more like upholstery department than a woman. Alexandra had better fortune in the slim shape of her refined and elegant mother, Princess Christian, from whom she learnt much of her style.

The relative poverty of Prince Christian, kept on a small income despite his position as heir to the Danish throne, was no disadvantage to his daughters' dress sense since it imposed on them the discipline of a very small budget for clothes and taught them by direct methods the need for quality in cut and cloth. Since Alexandra could not afford many clothes she had learnt to co-ordinate them, as she explained to Queen Victoria on her engagement visit to Osborne, when, as quoted in David Duff's *Alexandra, Princess and Queen*, Her Majesty enquired why she always wore a jacket at breakfast. 'I like them,' Alexandra is supposed to have said, 'and then, you see, a jacket is so economical. You can wear different skirts with it, and I have very few gowns, having to make them all myself. My sister and I have no lady's maid and have been brought up to make all our own clothes. I made my own bonnet.'

The professionalism of the Princess's millinery impressed several, including Princess Victoria's ex-lady-in-waiting, the delightfully-named Walpurga Paget, who took note of Alexandra's appearance as she said goodbye in Copenhagen before setting out to Gravesend: 'She wore a dress of brown silk with white stripes, and one of those natty little bonnets she used to make herself which seemed to sit better on her head than anybody else's. Even in those early days I was struck by the extreme neatness and taste of her attire.'

Neatness was another lady-like attribute only developed by the absence of a maid. A girl sits up straighter, and keeps her dresses' hems more carefully out of the mud, when she has to brush and iron them herself. Ellen Terry's friend, Mrs Comyns Carr, remembered ruefully in her memoirs the chore of looking after her print summer dresses by herself in the late 1860s when 'every self-respecting maiden ironed her dress daily, unless she had a maid to do it for her, and frills took no end of a time'.

But it would be wrong to assume that Alexandra's reputation for elegance was entirely the result of natural beauty and her upbringing. Like most mistresses of fashion, she worked at her looks, and did not let her individuality be swamped by the conventions by which she dressed. Like most mistresses of fashion, however sweet their exteriors, she had not only resources of determination but at times a spark of ruthlessness.

It was determination – or stubbornness – which produced the graceful, strangely gliding walk for which she was well known in her later years. Rheumatic fever after the birth of her third child in 1867 left her thinner still, with dark-circled eyes and faced at the age of twenty-three with a limp which threatened to curtail the dancing and riding she loved. Only hard practice brought it under control. Rarely without a stick, she had evening sticks made with jewelled handles, and defect was in her case so gracefully turned to advantage that ladies of the court were said in the early 1870s to be limping in imitation.

Whether it was from ruthlessness, a lack of thoughtfulness, an excess of Victorian sentimentality or some mixture of them all, it is the case that the women in her family circle were more overshadowed by her beauty than they need have been. Her sister Dagmar, for example, married to the heir to the throne of Russia and as passionate about clothes as Alexandra, was much the plainer of the pair: when, in 1873, she visited her in England and the two dressed in identical clothes for effect, it was Alexandra who benefited from the inevitable comparisons. Her daughters, none of them as lovely as their mother, were mercilessly dressed to match each other in the '80s, forming a gawky background to the charms of their mama. Her daughter-in-law fell victim to the same trap, and appeared at the Duchess of Devonshire's famous costume ball in 1897 as a mere 'Lady of the Court of . . .' to Alexandra's Queen Marguerite de Valois.

At least once there is an unambiguous case of out-manoeuvring on Alexandra's part. As Queen, she misled the ladies of her household about the timing of a change from full to half-mourning, and appeared for dinner spectacular in white while her ladies formed an indistinguishable – and indignant – black mass behind her. Scene-stealing is a relatively harmless vice, and as nothing compared to the Princess's abundant virtues which were apparent in her dress as well as her behaviour. She did not, like Eugénie, display a great devotion to high fashion; a tendency which was condemned by the mid-Victorians not as bad taste but as a sin. Many a stern paterfamilias reminded his daughter that women, in the words of Paul the apostle (I Timothy 2, ix-x), should 'adorn themselves in modest apparel, with shamefacedness and sobriety; not with broided hair, or gold, or pearls, or costly array; but (which becometh women professing godliness) with good works'.

Alexandra, particularly in her later years when she was devoted to charities as well as to the High Church, had a distaste for extravagant spending on finery: a truly gentlewomanly thriftiness. Not only did she have a brocade dress of hers unpicked and used to cover chairs at Sandringham, but she trained her daughters to make their own clothes. In March 1887, *The Lady's World* reported that a room had been set up at Sandringham with sewing machines for the use of the three young princesses.

In terms of a princess's wardrobe, or a queen's, thriftiness is of course a very relative matter, and Alexandra, like other Victorian wives, had a duty to dress for her husband as well as for her God. The importance of a woman's duty as a decorative object was well recognised by the fashion guides of the period. For an evening at home, for example, *The Art of Dressing Well and The Laws of Good Society* (published in 1875) decrees that 'the younger ladies of the family may . . . indulge their taste to the full. It is their place to brighten the drawing-room by their appearance, as well as by their accomplishments.' (Antiquated as this sounds, it is not so distant from the advice commonly handed out by women's magazines in the 1950s, suggesting that the dutiful wife should make an effort to slip out of head-scarf and rollers into something pretty in order to brighten her husband's return from his office.) While a husband might resent his wife appearing in highly fashionable dress, on the grounds that it suggests unmatronly flightiness as well as a spendthrift nature, dowdy dress on the other hand implied that his means were limited.

In the 1860s it was not too difficult for the well-dressed gentlewoman of Britain to remain camped well behind the front lines of fashion, for London was in any case a couple of years behind Paris. But even in the 1890s, when Paris and London modes were more closely synchronised, Consuelo, Duchess of Marlborough, discovered that she was expected to dress sumptuously rather than high-stylishly. 'Any extravagance of "fashion" was condemned as bad taste,' she remembered in her biography, *The Glitter and the Gold*, 'and no well-bred woman could afford to look seductive, at least not in public.'

To look attractive and prosperous, rather than spendthrift and sexy, is a business which calls for a delicate sense of balance. But if the ladies of Society ever felt disheartened by its complexities, they had only to look to the Princess of Wales for an example they could prudently follow. She took no risks. 'We have no safer guide to the best style and fashion in dress than HRH the Princess of Wales,' said the middle-class *Queen* – 'the Lady's newspaper' – in March 1880, before describing the black costume of cashmere and silk she had worn to a press view of

'Graphic Beauties': a black velvet jacket with trimming and muff of deep sable tail, appropriate to rank, a skirt a little looser than the mode, the bonnet very small in the Princess's usual style.

Her wedding dress had set a pattern for the discretion she was to display all her life. In 1863 crinolines were dangerously wide and accidents were common. The gently-born Lady Lucy and Lady Charlotte Bridgman had perished in a fiery sororial embrace before the library grate of Weston Hall, after one girl's crinoline had caught fire and the other had bravely attempted to put it out. Queen Victoria was strongly anti-crinoline, resenting having her subjects burn to death in Eugénie's ridiculous contraption, and Alexandra's English-made wedding dress had a skirt of very moderate circumference. Similar caution was used at the next great fashion shift, when the crinoline was finally out-moded in 1866, and the shape of hips and legs accordingly re-discovered; Alexandra obediently discarded her cage crinoline but wore demurely full, massed petticoats to swell out the bell of her skirts.

Not only did she avoid indelicacy and untidiness in her own clothes, she frowned on it in others. When, in 1880, there was a vogue for very skimpy sleeve-tops on formal evening dress, a mere strip of ribbon across the top of the arm, she banned such dresses from her balls at Marlborough House (the Wales' town residence) and for good measure forbade a new girlish hair-style of the locks tumbling loosely down the back instead of being (like Alexandra's in the '80s) primly pinned up. After a few waltzes, hair worn in such an unconstrained manner became hoydenishly tangled as well as improperly sexy. (So closely associated was loose hair with loose behaviour that Victorian novelists need only refer to a woman's hair coming down in the presence of a man for all kinds of passionate conclusions to be drawn by the reader.) Also, such a style, like the immodest sleeve-tops, was most becoming to very young women, and this at a time when the middle-aged Prince of Wales was conducting a succession of affairs with some of the pretty girls he danced with in his own ballroom beneath his wife's eye: maintaining the appearance of propriety in her social circles as well as in her dress was another of Alexandra's tricky tasks.

The well-dressed gentlewoman's evening dress, since it cannot be revealingly simple and skimpy, often depends instead on the naive attractions of girlish frills, such innocent ostentation being partly intended to display a husband's status. In her private dress, for her own occupations in the house and outside, the gentlewoman's costume is much more simple. Alexandra frequently dressed for public events in a

H.R.H. THE PRINCESS MARY OF TECK   H.R.H. THE DUCHESS OF EDINBURGH   H.R.H. THE PRINCESS LOUIS OF HESSE   H.R.H. THE PRINCESS OF WALES   H.R.H. THE PRINCESS CHRISTIAN

THE PRINCESSES

THE SCOTCH REEL

SOME OF THE COSTUMES

STATE BALL AT BUCKINGHAM PALACE

heavily ornamented way (though her grace of face and carriage ensured that her flounces did not overwhelm her) which horrified, for example, the sophisticated Jean Worth. His judgement of her appearance on a visit to Paris in 1878 in a court train deeply flounced with lace was that 'she looked for all the world like a maid decked out in her mistress's cast-off finery on her afternoon off'; the same kind of criticism was to be made again, a little over a century on, of the present Princess of Wales's preference for frills for evening and afternoon public engagements. But obvious prettiness has its romantic charms – though not, perhaps, to a man-milliner whose family firm has been passed over in favour of other Parisian couturiers. The Prince of Wales, himself a dandy with strong ideas on women's dress, was in favour of the obvious effect, especially in the display of rank, rebuking slips of etiquette in those around him. 'The Princess has taken the trouble to wear a tiara. Why have you not done so?' he once asked Consuelo, when as Duchess of Marlborough she had only decked her head with the diamond crescent fashionable in the 1890s.

The display of rank in costume and in jewellery was one of the important duties of an obedient wife, for it was her husband's and not her own position, family honour and riches which she was representing. It could be an onerous task, especially for those women whose own taste ran to the simple, but it was recognised by everyone. Wally Paget (as she was known to friends) was surprised to see the newly married Lady Dudley – formerly Georgiana Moncrieffe, the beauty of the seasons of 1864 and 1865 and after her marriage a nationally known Society beauty through the '70s – at a ball dressed only 'in a little pink gauze frock, with rosebuds in her hair, and not a single jewel' when it was well known that Lord Dudley had generously provided his bride with gems. It was a fault which Lord Dudley, who had particularly strong feelings about women's dress, soon remedied. Within a couple of years Lady Dudley's obligations lay literally heavily upon her. By the early 1870s she was to be found at her country house parties appearing each day in a new set of glittering jewels, which, by her husband's

3   Elaborate and conservative evening dress was expected of princesses. Those in the top row, and top rank, are more heavily flounced and bedecked than those unnamed and more fashionable exquisites in the bottom row. The Princess of Wales, in 1875 and at the height of her influence, is already well-known for her black velvet choker, but in the ballroom she is displaying rank, not the latest mode. Engravings like this from the illustrated papers gave female readers some clues to copy.

13

orders, she had to keep on until the evening, when she changed into more magnificent rocks. Fortunately for her reputation as a woman of taste, they were soon stolen at a railway station and never heard of again.

Alexandra, whose sloping shoulders and long, narrow neck made her an ideal display unit for royal jewels, was evidently more submissive than the young Georgiana Dudley, for she appeared in some sparkling piece for all her full-dress engagements immediately after her marriage, achieving a compromise between princely splendour and the fashionable girlish simplicity of the 1860s by twisting gems amongst the flowers wreathed round her hair. At a Marlborough House ball in the summer of her wedding year, for example, she wore diamonds and white roses as a wreath, and an emerald and diamond necklace to match a virginal dress of white glacé silk, veiled with spotted tulle and trimmed with white roses.

Which was more important in a toilette, the dress or the jewels, was not an easy question to answer. As late as the 1930s, Society dressmakers expected each vendeuse (who looked after particular clients who patronised the house) to be familiar with the heirloom pieces in her ladies' families and to suggest only evening dresses which could be worn with them. It would be a faux pas of the first order to propose a fuchsia gown for milady's ball and to be faced with an astonished 'But what about the *rubies*?' delivered in Lady Bracknell tones. That Alexandra's personal preference was to subordinate jewellery to gowns is suggested by the fact that she was, in later life, a keen buyer of Parisian fakes. Her own favourite piece in late middle age was a snake bracelet which writhed around her arm – amusing, but hardly ostentatious – and she wore very little jewellery during the day.

That Alexandra loaded herself with an ever-spreading armour of jewellery for evening engagements may be partly explained by Victoria's failure to take her place at the centre of London's social life. Alexandra compensated for the absence of a queen by being a particularly glittering Princess of Wales, and she did not undertake her social duties only for the sake of the aristocracy. However mistakenly, Alexandra – and Society – believed that the finery and social entertainments of 'the season' benefited the nation, supplying employment to tradespeople. The press shared this view, and the Prince and Princess of Wales were felt to be doing not just the pleasurable but the honourable thing in supplying a focus for the gaieties of the 'Upper Ten Thousand', as Society was vulgarly known to those outside it.

14

When the Prince of Wales left for India in 1875, the *World* lugubriously predicted six months of 'a sort of social stagnation and something very like complete paralysis to trade in the most fashionable quarters of London'. The *World*, as a Society rag, might be expected to take such a view, but there is evidence that tradesmen also valued the display of rank: in the mid-1880s Birmingham jewellers, suffering from a recession due to the fashion for very simple day dressing, appealed to Alexandra to bring the wearing of jewellery during the day back into fashion in order to save them. Nobly, she and her daughters sacrificed their uncluttered appearance in the cause but Alexandra was as unsuccessful as Canute in the matter of turning the tide. Again, in 1901, it was not the nobility but trade which objected at a reduction in display. The proposal of the newly acceded Edward VII, that the custom of wearing specially long, ornate court trains for Drawing Rooms should be limited to those debutantes and newly married women making their presentation curtseys, was greeted with relief by those who had to spend vast sums on an article which was worn only once and was afterwards useless (though one inventive peeress was said to have used a red velvet one of hers as a cover for her grand piano). It was the court dressmakers who prophesied misery and unemployment and had the decision reversed.

Obligations of this sort to tradesmen, and others to Society, husband and personal vanity, demanded the sacrifice of many woman-hours. The lady of Society was not free to spend all of her time as she wished. In addition to the hours allotted to the brushing and dressing of hair – it was put up at least twice a day in the 1860s and brushed for up to a hundred strokes, though photographs of the period suggest that it was not washed with quite such regularity – and time spent changing at least twice a day, and more often for sports or visits, there was the labour involved in the purchase of a new wardrobe for every season. Because none of it was ready-to-wear, many hours were spent standing perfectly still while circling dressmakers made measurements and stuck in pins. One of the advantages of patronising the best couturiers was that their skills in fitting enabled them to demand fewer sessions. The worst might take four for each dress – and a great many dresses were needed. 'The season', Society's time in London with a packed calendar of social events, lasted in the early 1870s from the beginning of May to the end of July. In France, Eugénie had set a precedent by wearing a dress only once to a public engagement. How closely this was followed in London is impossible to say, but Society did expect a constant parade of new outfits from those of rank. Millicent, Duchess of Sutherland, a beauty of the 1890s, kept in her late (and poorer) middle age the ingrained habit of wearing an evening dress only twice before giving it away. That Alexandra would, if it were possible given her position at the top of Society, have found a way of squeezing extra wear out of her dresses is suggested by the that she made her maids darn her stockings; her very wedding dress, in the care of the London Museum of Costume, has been unsentimentally altered for extra use. But the most imaginative re-cycling can have made little impact on the weeks involved in assembling a wardrobe of new dresses and accessories: hats, gloves, fans, shoes, furs, parasols, sticks, minor jewellery and the rest.

Then there was the pyramid of servants with minor or major duties relating to a lady's clothes, the most time-consuming – or employment-producing, depending on your view – being the job of laundering. Washing, boiling, starching and ironing underclothes and the few washable garments a lady wore took up the full time of skilled laundry staff. Miss Annie Wilkinson, interviewed in 1968 for *Costume* magazine, recalled that in her youth it took a whole day standing without a break from 9 till 5 to iron one court petticoat: 'The train on it took me an hour to go round with the goffers.'

At the top of the pyramid, also with her whole time taken up by the labours attendant upon her mistress's wardrobe, was the lady's maid, a creature who is nowadays rarer but by no means extinct. Princess Michael of Kent has been quoted as saying wistfully that the best-dressed women she knows have maids, or dressers as the royal family calls them. For the woman of rank who wished to play a conventional rôle in the society of Victoria's time a maid was a necessity. A good maid could almost take the place of the long stare in the long mirror recommended by magazines of the 1930s to those who wished to appear properly neat from head to foot. It was the maid's place to ensure that all hems were straight, no spot or stain was showing anywhere, all was tidily adjusted, all hooks were done up and nothing had been forgotten. If a lady suddenly discovered halfway through the evening that her ears were naked of their rings, it was her maid and not herself she blamed.

It was the maid's duty to tie and hook and hitch her mistress's clothing into place and to do her hair. At the end of the day, she was expected to let her out of her garments and untangle the tiara from her locks. But the maid was not idle in the time between changes of dress: there were brushes and combs to clean, delicate laces and silks to wash which could not be trusted to the laundry, stains to remove by dry-cleaning methods from fine garments, the organising of the changes of dress for days ahead, the folding and storing and cosseting with lavender bags, the packing and listing and labelling, with sheets of tissue paper for travels, the brushing of mud-spattered riding habits, the preparation of ointments and lotions against freckles, spots and similar problems (the lady's maid was expected to have a few recipes for the commonest beauty maladies in her repertoire), the mending of her mistress's clothes and, if she had time free, the making of fine items of underwear and the like. There was also the great responsibility of looking after the jewels – listing them, sending them to be cleaned and mended and carrying them on travels, often in a third-class compartment.

Despite all this trouble in the cause of another's looks, a maid might be harshly treated. The American Jerome sisters, Clara, Leonie and Jennie – who married Lord Randolph Churchill – were all in the habit of throwing hair-brushes at their maids in moments of creative stress in front of the mirror. (Alexandra, whose natural tidiness must have made her light work, was exceptionally kind to her maids. Her first, Louisa Jones, she nursed through a typhoid illness until Louisa died in her mistress's arms.) But despite the disadvantages of long hours and the frequently difficult mistress, a maid's was a sought-after job, involving close and prestigious contact with the family, travel and fine clothes, many of which came her way from the lady's wardrobe as part of the perks of the job and which, though they could not be worn in her presence, could be profitably sold.

If the maid's mistress was a recognised beauty or a leader of fashion, there was also the enjoyment of sharing in her triumph, for the finished product of all these woman-hours could be very influential. Society was so small, and so frequently meeting in its fixed and formal rounds, that a woman with a reputation for dress could constantly set trends. Her imitators followed her example not only deliberately but unconsciously – it need be only a vague memory which makes a woman choose a shade of cinnamon for herself which she has seen look well on someone else. A glance and an impression of good effect are all that is needed.

Alexandra was admired because of her elegance and beauty, but she was also copied because she had been successful at the sport of husband-hunting and had carried off the chief prize – the Prince of Wales. Those of her contemporaries who dressed with the same lady-like aims copied her style the most closely: they studied her ball gowns at the private balls which occupied the evenings throughout the London season, her spotless riding habits in Rotten Row, her small feathered hats and smart, simple jackets for driving in Hyde Park, her beribboned dresses for Hurlingham in late May and Ascot in June, her mannish suits for Cowes in August.

Some of Alexandra's imitators were more loyal than wise. Like most leaders of fashion she exaggerated her best features, and women who thoughtlessly followed her example could find themselves highlighting their own worst aspects. Her long, narrow neck and proudly-held head, for example, were well displayed by the upstanding Medici collar of the 1880s (it was a feature of her Coronation dress in 1902) but it was a mode which made the thick-necked or double-chinned look ridiculous. The same applied to most of Alexandra's best-known hallmarks, which all directed attention to her face: her chokers and her tiny hats, for example. None were fashions that she initiated, for the Princess of Wales was not original in thought, but they were popularised by her preference for them. Chokers, which were more associated with her than any other item of apparel, were already worn in Paris in the 1860s. When, with the adoption of dress with eighteenth-century echoes in the 1870s, the eighteenth-century choker seemed a natural accessory and was accepted generally, Princess Alexandra was quick to see its advantages. Not only would it hide the slight scar on her neck, but it emphasised a small neck. In the early 1870s she favoured black velvet chokers, which could dramatically set off diamonds or pendant pearls, but by 1880 she was wearing pearls alone wound round her throat. That season most of the young women in Society could be seen to sport a double row with evening dress, sometimes worn over lace.

A series of pregnancies throughout the 1860s (she had six children between January 1864 and April 1871) prevented the Princess from being as influential on the fashions of that time as she was later in the 1870s and 1880s. Mrs Comyns Carr describes her as 'the accepted leader' of fashion in the late 1870s, with a marked effect on modes, particularly hats: 'Perhaps the most popular fashion ever set by the Princess was the small, flat headgear which, about that time, was substituted for the most ornate form of bonnet. On her graceful head it was charming, but it was unhesitatingly adopted by all Society, without any consideration of becomingness.' It was a criticism repeatedly made of the Gadarene Swine school of dressers.

One important fashion which the Princess popularised did suit almost everyone. It was a garment which was at once perfectly English and supremely lady-like, and was to become the staple of the classic dresser over the next century: the tailored suit. Alexandra held all the necessary advantages with which to display the quality of British tailor-

18

ing, including an excellent figure and a graceful, upright carriage. Ball gowns which have survived would have been closely fitted to her body and still reveal her shape like a plaster mould: the held-back shoulders and the pulled-in waist. Part of the reason for her continuing slimness and suppleness, which amazed her peers, was the Princess's addiction to sport and activity, to riding, to skating, to dancing, to romping with her children – she was not too stiff to join in soda-siphon battles with her sons. Long before those who pursued beauty also forced themselves to chase fitness, Alexandra took an unquenchable joy in movement for its own sake, undeterred by lameness or age. And it was through sport that the suit became popular, just as it was through the increasingly active sports open to women that their dress gradually became freer as the century progressed.

From the beginning of the Princess's time in England her clothes – those jackets Victoria had wondered about – were seen to be young and sporty. Skirts and jackets, topped by flat hats with feathers, were the correct dress for walking and for croquet and general outdoor pursuits. A bright manufacturer, probably picking up the Princess's preference from a photograph published before the wedding, explained in an advertisement on the eve of the royal wedding the uses to which 'The Alexandra Jacket' might be put. With a long, loose line and peg-top sleeves, it was 'suitable for the garden, country walks, picnics, boating, as an over-jacket in riding and for indoors on a cold day'. It was the usual outdoor wear for young women of the upper classes during the days spent at their country estates, but it was evidently not very familiar to the bulk of the readership of the *Illustrated London News*: the town-based middle classes. By 1867 this loose jacket, its royal connection explicitly made, is mentioned in *Queen* as 'definitely adopted for morning outdoor wear' in town. It had other uses which must have been particularly welcome to Alexandra in those years for, with its non-fitted waist, it was ideally suited to pregnancy.

Packed amongst the trousseau Alexandra brought to England in 1863 was such a jacket, and a skirt for one of the fashionable and social sports of the time: croquet. In half-mourning colours, like the whole trousseau (Alexandra spent a large portion of her life in mourning for one royal relative or another, so it was fortunate that violet and grey suited her as well as they did), the jacket was of cream flannel with a decorative trimming of cream lace over mauve ribbon round its mandarin collar, and ribbon and lace appliqué down the front. It would have been worn at a 3 pm croquet party, one of the few outdoor gatherings at which

4   In fancy dress as in all evening wear, Alexandra was expected to provide a show of splendour. This purple-red gown, worn at a fancy dress ball at Marlborough House in 1874, is that of a Venetian lady, but it incorporates Alexandra's favourite tip-tilted head-dress and her pearl-hung, lace and velvet choker.

Victorian girls might fulfil more than a decorative rôle (archery was another), though the functional shortening of their crinolines had the paradoxical effect of making them more decorative than ever. It is easier to see why young Victorians had such enthusiasm for the apparently decorous game of croquet when it is remembered how easily cage crinolines swung up to reveal the wearer's legs. To take advantage of this, the croquet-player's stockings were coloured and decorated, and her knee-length drawers fancily edged.

Over the short crinoline the skirts were looped up to reveal a

20

5 Typical of the carte-de-visites which told a fascinated public how photogenic their new Princess of Wales was – and what kind of clothes she wore. This photograph, taken at Abergeldie in the year of her marriage, 1863, shows how composed Alexandra already was in front of a camera. She is wearing a walking crinoline, looped up to show a decorative petticoat and with a favourite loose jacket, very similar to the dress she would have worn for croquet. The small, tip-tilted hat became one of her hallmarks: the one here is seen again in other photographs, revealing that Alexandra was more thrifty in her wardrobe than was the Empress Eugénie, who was said to wear a ballgown only once.

Her patriotic tartan must have gladdened the hearts of the Scots as much as the present Princess of Wales did when she presented herself at the Braemar Games in her first year of marriage, 1981, in an all-tartan suit.

decorative petticoat, a fashion Alison Gernsheim attributes to the influence of Pauline von Metternich in 1859. Looped-up skirts over short crinolines were also worn in the early 1860s as walking dress. By the mid-1860s the skirt was looped up at the back instead of being evenly gathered all round, and by the end of the '60s everyday fashion had followed suit.

But it was not on the croquet lawn or in the country lane that maximum liberty was allowed the Victorian girl and reflected in her dress; it was not, in fact, on dry land at all. Boating gave the most freedom from chaperones and the least restrictive, most practical dress. Of punting, boating and yachting the latter was the most prestigious and it was the adoption for it of dark, mannish, tailored suits which most quickly popularised them. At Cowes the Princess of Wales might be seen on the royal yacht in the early 1870s in daring boater, a squarish jacket and matching skirt of dark cloth, drawn into a slight bustle at the back. She looked comfortable, superbly simply dressed, and unmistakably feminine.

The Princess's unquestioningly traditional womanly subservience was a great asset to the popular acceptance of the manly suit, which common prejudice associated with intellectual, unfeminine women – the sort of thing women at the new Oxbridge Halls might be expected to wear. In the early '70s the tweedy country suits which had evolved from the plain jackets and skirts of the '60s, and the long belted overcoat of rough material, so sensible for country wear and known as the ulster because it originated in that country, were condemned as fast and mannish, two adjectives frequently coupled together, but the Princess of Wales was pretty and gentle enough to carry them off without either criticism. As a result Alexandra, in the country at least, was ahead of Eugénie, for the French, less closely involved with their country estates than the bucolic English, had not evolved a practical style of dress to wear in it. Jennie Jerome, who came from Paris to England in 1874 for her marriage to Lord Randolph Churchill with cases full of the plumed hats and Louis XV heels the French thought chic for country wear, had, she said, 'many bitter experiences with long gown and thin, paper-like shoes before realising the advantages of short skirts and "beetle-crushers"'. In functional tailor-mades the British combination of expert tailoring and practical experience of country and sporting matters led the world.

The most prestigious tailor for women, whose name was inextricably linked with Alexandra's, was Redfern, whose tailor-mades were seen in towns as well as in the country in the late '70s. By 1888, dark tailor-made suits were acceptable wear for tea at Hurlingham (not a stamping ground for intellectuals) if the weather were bad, and Redfern had branches in Paris and New York as well as London and Cowes, proclaiming the patronage of the Princess of Wales at each shop. The classic garment of the lady-like had been firmly established for its future.

But for those women in Society who did not wish to follow the lady-like, the family-minded and the country-based, there were always other models to follow. In the 1860s those who preferred the dashing to the decorous looked to the Duchess of Manchester for a lead. Older than Alexandra (she was thirty-one in 1863 and reckoned to be at the peak of her forceful beauty), she was ambitious, political, cunning, intelligent and notoriously unfaithful to her husband. She swiftly established herself in the circle of the young Prince of Wales's most amusing friends, to Queen Victoria's alarm. Blonde and heavy-featured, she

6   The dashing Duchess of Manchester, highly fashionable and very strong-willed, photographed by Camille Silvy in about 1863. Despite her girlish wreath of flowers and slightly parted lips, she does not look pretty. The photograph must have come as a disappointment to those who had heard of the Duchess's reputation as a beauty. Note how tensely she holds herself, compared to Alexandra, and the elaborate setting, which is far grander than anything Silvy created for his other clients at that period. Pearls at neck, ears and waist display her status, as does the huge flounce of old lace. The Duchess, despite the disadvantages of too-square shoulders and claw-like hands, managed by intelligence and determination to lead fashion for a couple more decades. Even in the 1890s it was considered that the Duchess (by then of Devonshire) was worthy of having her dresses reported in Society magazines: she was then in her sixties.

dressed in high fashion with intent to allure, and continued to do so after her daughters came of age – though she was criticised for her adoption of French modes in the English countryside. In the '70s she reminded the future Lady Ottoline Morrell, peeping over the stairs of Welbeck at her mother's guests, of Bess of Hardwick: velvet-dressed, bejewelled, domineering.

In the '60s, however, the time was out of joint for the mistress of fashion whose reputation deserved the double entendre: the girlish colours and trims of the dresses looked odd upon them. The Duchess's strong, proud face was mis-matched by her crowning circlet of innocent flowers, and Lady Mary Craven, a reigning beauty in the ballrooms of the late '60s, with her known lover on her arm, paint on her face and russet dye on her hair, was inappropriately clothed in sweet pink satin trimmed with fringes of grass and innocent daisies. Alexandra was better suited to the fashions of the decade, and she should have made an even greater impact on them than she did. Her influence on dress was restricted not only because of her pregnancies but because a wider public than that of her social circle lacked information about her clothes.

In England there was not, as there was in France, a whole network of sketchers, fashion writers and pattern-makers ready to transmit the latest whims of Eugénie and the notables of her court, via the fashion columns of papers and magazines, throughout the fashionable world. In Paris fashion journalists roamed the races and the theatre, ready to scribble down details of toilettes not just of the French but of visiting Americans too. The French correspondent of *Queen* spotted Clara Jerome, Lady Randolph Churchill's elder sister, in 1869 in the Imperial Box of the Théâtre Français and she took down the trimming of the dress with more accuracy than the spelling of the surname: 'Miss Gerome, the American belle, wore a straw-coloured tarlatan dress, with tunic of rich straw silk, forming a round tablier in front, and trimmed with Chinese fringe, made of straw silk. Bodice tastefully ornamented with fringe. Round chaplet of tea roses.' This was typical of the detailed reports of dress which appeared in the Paris columns. There was no such coverage of English fashionables' dress, except an occasional note of a guest's dress at a Society wedding, or a line in the court circular on the costume of the Princess of Wales for a public appearance. Fashion magazines of the 1860s and 1870s offered their readers almost no guidance on what was worn by the British aristocracy, though there was some detail given in the court circulars of Alexandra's dress in the first season of her marriage.

Even the readers of the *Englishwoman's Domestic Magazine*, a solidly middle-class affair whose fashion correspondent was the famous Mrs Beeton, who must have been agog for news of the clothes of the new Princess in 1863, were treated only to a diatribe against foolish imitators, illustrated by a sketch of grotesques in greasy versions of Alexandra's hair-style: 'The new fashion of wearing the hair in those Alexandra ringlets, so charming when the two full rich tresses droop like silken snakes over a shoulder of ivory, [is] often too provocative of merriment, not to say contempt, when they fall like limp weeds upon a spare and sinewy neck or are remorselessly twisted into unyielding corkscrews.' The lack of coverage was a missed opportunity to boost not only circulation but the British textile trade and fashion business.

For the interest was there, as was demonstrated by the popularity of the corkscrews. Young women up and down the country had learned about them from one of the few sources available to them which gave proper details of Alexandra's appearance in 1863, the carte de visite photograph. Small – usually about 2¼ by 4 inches – thick, gilt-edged pieces of card, they were for sale in shops everywhere for 1d or 2d black and white, 4d or 6d coloured and by post at the time of the wedding for the high price of 1s 6d (7½p) plain black and white, or 3s (15p) coloured. Since in the '60s retouching was still an undeveloped art, a reputation for looks could fall with the shutter. The Duchess of Manchester, for instance, does not look well on hers. But, as the *Illustrated London News* proudly pronounced on 7 March 1863, the new Princess of Wales (the first since the invention of the camera) was photogenic in addition to all her other qualities. 'It is no flattery,' they justly said, 'to say that we have seen no "subject" pass the severe test of photography so triumphantly as Princess Alexandra.' Alexandra's image brushed cheeks with the family in albums throughout Britain. Photographs of her at first had the effect – as in the case of Lady Diana Spencer – of popularising her hair-style, but later photographs, which continued to sell in huge numbers, gave some information on her clothes. Photographs exist where the very pose of Alexandra with a child has been imitated, so it is at least probable that her dresses might also have had an effect on the taste of those who studied her image, particularly outside London, where there was least contact with sophisticated fashions. Not until 1880 was there written material in the fashion columns of *Queen* of any quality to help those in the provinces copy the Princess of Wales, although Londoners could gain some idea of her style, and the style of other ladies of Society, from the drives in Hyde Park during the season.

But the pious Victorians were not merely concerned with the influence of a woman's dress on the dress of others: they claimed greater moral powers for it. 'A woman is more or less judged by the style of her dress and further,' *The Art of Dressing Well etc* instructed the gentle-woman reader, 'half her influence for good or bad depends on it also.' In this respect the good and beautiful Princess must be said to have failed. Her loveliness and dress sense, though appreciated by the Prince of Wales (he told Wally Paget at a Marlborough House ball in the '60s, 'We have asked only the prettiest women in London, but the Princess is the most beautiful of them all'), had little effect on his morals.

It was possible to take claims for the good influence of beauty too far.

2
Professional Beauties

It was the Prince of Wales's roving eye which was partly responsible for the creation of that 1870s phenomenon, the Professional Beauty, or the PBs, as they were known in the plural. The Prince formed the mid-point of a circle of wealthy, middle-aged and under-occupied men anxious to be amused. As a result, any hostess who hoped for success must have on her party list a good selection of lively and lovely young women. 'The PBs will all be there' was a promise likely to ensure a better turn-out of guests. And the relative merits of the PBs themselves were discussed by their male fanciers almost as eagerly as were those of racehorses.

But thanks to the development of photography, their looks were also discussed quite familiarly outside Mayfair and beyond the estate gates of country mansions. By the 1870s photographs were bigger and photographers more ambitious. The cabinet photograph, introduced by 1866, was six inches by four inches, much larger than the carte de visite, and striking enough to display in shop windows. It also allowed studio special effects to be admired. The combination of these two circumstances created a demand for beautiful women to photograph.

Inevitably, Society provided them. Besides Princess Alexandra, Georgiana Dudley was among the very first faces to be propped up in High Street window displays. The PBs soon joined her there, and the Prince of Wales's reputation only added glamour to their names – much as Mick Jagger's reputation adds glamour to Jerry Hall's. In the 1870s the combination of Prince and photography resulted in a national craze for beauties almost as widespread as the 1930s craze for film stars.

Their fame made the PBs highly influential on fashion in looks and clothes, outside Society as well as within it. For the large cabinet photograph, besides allowing photographers to experiment by introducing live animals, stuffed birds, shepherdesses' crooks and so forth into the picture also allowed the viewer a much better idea of hair-style and details of dress. And the PBs' influence was not restricted to their contemporaries. They also had an influence on future generations, for

7 The Countess of Dudley, Society beauty throughout her life and a trend-setter in fashions of dress and behaviour. She was particularly admired for her very small head, her air of composure and her strictly simple elegance. Married to a man who had strong and peculiar ideas on the ideal dress for women, she carried out her function in his eyes as a decorative object superbly well. A cabinet taken by Downey in about 1880.

they were in many ways the forerunners of the pretty, clothes-horse actresses of the 1890s and early 1900s, and of today's model girls.

What marked them out from the handsome girls who cropped up in every generation in the best families, and who were famous in the ballrooms for a season, was their professionalism. PBs were not brilliantly born or solidly wealthy; they relied for their position at the top of Society's rounds almost entirely on their looks. By the late 1870s a beautiful wife was a well-known route up through the ranks for a social-climbing husband – so long as he was not too jealous. *Punch* ran several cartoons on the subject, including one which showed an ugly little man propelling his meal ticket into a party, her face lit either side with candles the better to display it.

The most successful of the PBs dressed deliberately to amuse and allure. Their styles and their faces were much compared, and so were those of the Society beauties who happened to live during their period, including Daisy Maynard, Violet Lindsay (Lady Diana Cooper's mother), Georgiana Dudley, Lady Randolph Churchill and many others. Each had her particular charms and distinctive style and a host of minor imitators. But the acknowledged Queen amongst the real PBs was beautiful Lillie Langtry, who rose from a modest, middle-class background to the highest position a PB could occupy.

It is tempting but wrong to suppose that Lillie simply happened to own a face which coincided with the taste of her time. Quite the contrary: the taste of the time had to be educated to appreciate Lillie's looks. When Lord Rosslyn, Daisy Maynard's Lord-about-town step-father, exhibited Mrs Langtry to his friends in her earliest days in London they mocked his claim that she was an exceptional looker. And Lillie herself was unimpressed. 'I am never surprised when people say that they are disappointed in my looks,' she said. 'I have never understood why they are admired.'

There was certainly nothing immediately striking about her. Memoir writers have handed down contradictory reports about her colouring. Daisy Warwick, as Daisy Maynard became, claimed that Lillie had violet eyes and a skin like a peach. Lillie herself said in her autobiography that she had naturally corn-coloured hair. Graham Robertson and Ellen Terry, who, unlike the other two, wrote their own memoirs, speak more convincingly of grey eyes and brown hair with glints of gold in it. Early photographs show a girl with large, light, calm eyes, a good profile made slightly heavy by a tendency to plumpness around the jaw-line, a large, fairly straight nose with a slight tilt at the end, a full mouth, excellent pale skin and a pair of large, ungainly hands. She was too firmly fleshed to photograph well, but even when allowances are made for the ungallant camera, it is necessary to agree with Ellen Terry that Lillie was an acquired taste.

Society acquired that taste through the 1870s' craze for the aesthetic, for Lillie was discovered, as many an amazed woman had been before her, by a group of enthusiastic artists who preferred a type of looks which was a little unusual. In the 1860s several women whose faces had previously been excused as unfortunate had suddenly discovered Rossetti and Swinburne sighing by their slippers. In the past they had become models and occasionally, like Jane Morris or Elizabeth Siddal, married an artist. But in 1875, when Lillie was stumbled upon, the combined excitement of Millais, Whistler, Henry Irving and Frank Miles over her Grecian face, her firm, sculptured features, her columnar

29

neck and the modest tilt of the head was expressed not in some middle-class garden in Clapton but in Lady Sebright's salon. Artists were fashionable: what they liked, Society must also admire. Society obediently saw Grecian traces in Lillie's face. They also, more enthusiastically, saw that her figure was excellent and her bust and arms, when exposed by formal evening dress, were beautifully moulded and extremely white.

Those outside Society, the ordinary people who massed on pavements outside balls or by Rotten Row to see the ladies ride by, were not always so willing to admire the fashionable when they saw famous beauties in the flesh.

Daisy, a Society beauty who received as much attention as many a PB, remembered in her memoirs being critically eyed by the mob after a rough voyage to Ireland in the early '80s. 'I was awakened by my mother's voice saying, "Get up, darling. The crowd is waiting to have a look at you." As I passed down the gangway, sure enough there was a crowd of people pressing close to see me, and I heard a woman say, "How can people be so ridiculous? She's *very* ugly."'

Later, Lillie compensated for any initial disappointment she aroused in her public by wearing very sumptuous clothes and jewels. But at her first London parties she was not particularly interested in clothes, and she had none of the tricks of dressing she later learnt. A tomboy girlhood, spent running wild with her brothers in Jersey, had given her more of a passion for practical jokes and racehorses than for finery. Fittings bored her. And she had never needed a social wardrobe: two morning dresses (i.e. day dresses) and one formal evening dress from her Jersey dressmaker, all in mourning black because of her brother's death, were all she had needed for the spring of 1875, or so she had thought before she became the rage of that season.

Society, amazed that she was constantly seen in the same dowdy black evening dress, had exaggerated notions of her poverty, which added to the interest they took in her: she was a curiosity. But Lillie was married to a man of independent means and had a lady's maid. She was not poor, just poorer than the class she now was to mix in.

Her wardrobe's lean stock and her complete lack of jewellery, however eccentric in the setting of Belgravia, were not uncommon amongst the genteel middle classes. Guides to dressing well within a moderate income for that period show that black was regarded as useful not just as conventional mourning dress but because it did not show age or spots, particularly in evening candlelight. It was common for one day

30

dress to be designed, as Lillie's was, with an adjustable neckline to turn it into a dinner dress so that a single sumptuous, low-necked, formal evening dress might be kept for best. Since houses in the '70s were still lit only by candles or gas, middle-class girls wishing to stretch their wardrobes had their new best dresses made as 'occasion' morning dresses where daylight was searching, for archery parties and so on. After a season's wear the morning dress could be converted into an evening dress with some clever re-making.

Because Lillie's evening dress was black she was able to wear it night after night, to several parties each evening. It was a fortunate chance that the colour showed off the whiteness of her skin, outlined her figure and made her hair, worn plaited and knotted back in a simple twist, look more golden. Lillie had discovered the charms of the Little Black Dress.

By a similar chance she had stumbled on another great weapon of the stylist, especially one who wishes to make her way in a strange society – the virtues of hallmark dressing. Lillie was instantly recognisable and easily remembered in a way that she would not have been had her dress varied. She even had a hallmark flower, from the shortened form of her name, Emilie, which was not only the pink flower of her island home but also one of the favourite symbols of the aesthetic movement. She was a modern PR man's dream.

Frank Miles's pictures of her and the lily made hallmark flowers a fashion. Strong-willed Daisy Maynard was sketched as a matter of course in the early '80s by Frank Miles with her quite inappropriate flower by her debutante face. She wore daisies as buttons on her dress and as prints on her summer chiffons. When she married the Earl of Warwick's heir, she gave her bridesmaids memento jewellery in the form of coroneted daisies. Even Princess Alexandra had a flower: she adopted the royal red rose, which she wore pinned by her long throat.

But besides giving Lillie the perfect logo and an ideal uniform, fate provided her with the ultimate publicist in the person of Oscar Wilde. His Oxford first in classics provided him with a fund of quotes with which to praise Lillie's Grecian beauties, and when the black dress had at last been abandoned, it was his aesthetic eye which helped her choose effective, classical-looking gowns. The pair sometimes went to parties dressed to tone.

If it was fate which made Lillie famous at first, it was her own energy and intelligence which made her the most successful of the PBs and ensured that she would not be forgotten. Among her interesting qualities which had been overlooked at Lady Sebright's were her sharp mind, her commercial aptitude and her independent nature. As a result it did not take Lillie long to see, analyse and exploit the reasons for her popularity.

At the end of Lillie's first season Lady Dudley gave a ball. That same Lord who had earlier forced his wife to wear glittering quantities of gems in daylight had a prejudice against morbid clothes like Lillie's black dress, but a party without Lillie was unthinkable. Ostensibly to solve Lady Dudley's dilemma, Lillie went to a London dressmaker for the first time. Her entrance to the ball in expertly-cut lily-white velvet with pearl embroidery caused the intended sensation. The hallmark black had served its turn. Lillie was known to all, and her talent for a long career as a Professional Beauty began to be evident.

She had other companions in mischief besides Oscar Wilde. Professional beauties flourish best in the company of others. Camaraderie, competition and publicity are all advantages, especially if the beauties complement each other by contrast. Blonde, strong-faced Jerry Hall was frequently seen in the 1970s with the dark-haired, delicate-featured Marie Helvin. Lillie's equivalent friend was Mary Cornwallis-West, a romping Irish girl of twenty-one who was married to a man of limited riches twenty-two years her senior. Slim, small, with cropped blonde curly hair, a long straight nose, a wide mouth, pronounced cheek-bones, a high colouring and large brown eyes, she had a vitality and humour to match Lillie's. Sliding downstairs at country house parties on tea trays was only one of the sports they both enjoyed. Not a romp, but a fellow PB, was Mrs Wheeler, whose dark hair, grey eyes, beauty of expression and reserve were an acquired taste. She was most admired for her originality, for she had turned down the Prince of Wales.

Connoisseurs endlessly compared the PBs' rival attractions and talked of new discoveries, and the PBs took great pride in their status. They were careful of their reputation for looks, if not for virtue. As a result, although artifice might have been expected to be more acceptable to the professional beauty than to the lady-like, it does not seem to have been. The PBs took suggestions that they needed to wear make-up as an affront to their pride. Mary Cornwallis-West washed her face in public one Ascot to prove the natural origin of her high colouring after hearing a passing stranger remark that it was a shame she painted. Lillie wore no make-up in her youth at all. Yet among Society's best-bred, false complexions were quite general. According to the sophisticated correspondent of the *World* on 20 October 1875, make-up of a crude kind

8   When the era of Professional Beauties began in the mid-1870s, photographers began to experiment with special effects. This photograph of Mary Cornwallis-West is so carefully arranged that it could almost be a *Vogue* fashion photograph of the next century. Mary – short-haired, lively and notoriously ready for any kind of practical joke – would not have taken much persuading to arrange herself with furs, dog, sleigh and artificial snow in a photographer's studio. Pictures like this of the PBs were keenly collected, and those who starred in them were stared at and mobbed in the street like latter-day film stars.

33

9 Mrs Wheeler, from a supplement to *Society* in November 1883. Of all the PBs, Mrs Wheeler was most famous for her discretion and her determination: she turned down the Prince of Wales, who was not slow to spread the news of his astounding rejection. Those who preferred Mrs Wheeler's face claimed that she was less obvious but more interesting in her appeal than the rowdier PBs. Her beauty lay in sweetness of expression and in its reserve.

(powder, kohl and lip-salve as well as rouge) was to be seen in every ballroom, inexpertly applied. He blamed it on the influence of seeing male relatives openly parading with painted whores.

If the PB's face was not highly-coloured, her dress was usually in the height of fashion. Once Lillie had left behind her black, and embarked on a series of affairs, her dress changed to a butterfly mode and a butterfly motif. 'My only purpose in life,' she wrote in her memoirs, 'being to look nice and make myself agreeable.' She made herself especially agreeable to the Prince of Wales. For a ball at his London home, Marlborough House, she wore a dress of 'yellow tulle, draped with wide-meshed gold fish-net in which preserved butterflies of every hue and size were held in glittering captivity' – but not held securely enough, according to her memoirs. The following morning a plumply sentimental, enthralled Prince wandered across an empty ballroom, gathering the fallen mementoes of his love's progress. At a private view at the Grosvenor Gallery in 1880 Lillie was seen in a costume of black satin, the hood of her mantle lined with crimson and gold and trimmed with gold butterflies with green and blue wings, worn with a black and gold bonnet. The Little Black Dress had been replaced by an altogether more elaborate mode. It was witty, but not eccentric. Despite her aesthetic beginnings Lillie wore conventional undergarments and conventional cuts. But it was elaborate, and it was expensive.

The cost of dressing to match the PB status was, however, not entirely carried by the PB's husband. Dressmakers helped by giving long credit and good reductions, even free garments. Lillie had especially good terms because of her known liaison with royalty, and also because of the commercial value of her patronage. Other men also helped. Though the PBs had affairs rather than being 'kept', they were certainly not too proud to accept gifts of clothes or jewellery from lovers or mere admirers. Though she did not, like the lady-like dresser, have to display the wealth and status of her husband, the PB might well display the wealth of other women's. Mary Cornwallis-West was given a witty hat by the Duke of Fife, intended to attract the attention a lady-like dresser shuns: 'It was made of a ptarmigan, the head of which stuck out in front so that when she put it on her head it gave the impression of the bird sitting on a nest,' remembered her son, George Cornwallis-West.

When Lillie met Disraeli, who politely asked what he could do for her, she promptly requested four new dresses for Ascot. And Baron Ferdinand de Rothschild offered a whole group of ten PBs new gowns from the couturier Doucet to wear at his ball. It was a cynical gift, made in the same spirit as an order to the florist for decorations. The problem was that his all-white ballroom, well lit, revealed all the grease-marks and stains on ballgowns that ladies were accustomed to have lost in the shadows, and the Baron wanted the spectacle of his ball to be of the best quality. Lillie took the dress, not offence, and, by then no slouch at the game, ordered an extra petticoat from the dressmaker; she was furious when the Baron refused to pay for it. The Prince of Wales was in the habit of taking his fancy of the moment to Paris incognito and picking up large bills from a grateful Worth at the end of the visit.

Whimsical, mercurial high fashion was perfect for the PB. Its extravagances emphasised her function as a toy. The beauty's dress was not only elaborate, it was deliberately provocative, as, to contemporary eyes, was the dress of her period. Wally Paget mused smugly on the outrage her chaperones of the 1860s would have felt could they but have seen the evening dress of 1883. 'Ye gods! If they could see our present clinging robes and the bodices held up by a strap and a flower!' None wore more clinging robes than Lillie. For her Redfern made a sheath-like jersey top which stretched to every contour in such a fashion that *Punch* in caricature compared it to the wearing of underwear in public. It was launched by Lillie at the Cowes Regatta of August 1879, but her fame at once popularised and killed it. Word of the new fashion reached the middle-class wife's housemaid so quickly that her mistress had been forced to discard it by the following spring.

By the late 1870s London was more of a social and fashionable capital than it had been in the previous decade. The Franco-Prussian war had deprived Paris of its Empress just as the Prince and Princess of Wales had firmly established their own busy and amusing social circles on the other side of the Channel. It is no coincidence that it is in this period of Eugénie's exile that Alexandra can be so easily seen to be influencing the genteel fashion of English Society, or that Langtry's lead in shoes, hats and dresses was so eagerly followed. Even American heiresses began to spend the season in the British capital. London dressmakers were also becoming better known, but the label was still far from being as important as its wearer, and the designer was nothing more than a tradesman, certainly not an artist. Lady Randolph Churchill remembered 'laughing immoderately' at breakfast during a shooting party at Blenheim when one Lady Wilton appeared in an electric-blue velvet and, on being asked who made it, said with conscious pride, 'It's a Stratton' as she would say, 'It's a Van Dyck.'

The established, busy social life in London gave the PBs and their

10 A rare outdoor, un-retouched shot of Lillie Langtry, seen here with Millais, in the closely-fitting, simple outdoor dress she was famous for in the late 1870s. Perfectly tailored, with rows of buttons to outline her shape, it attracts attention to Lillie's figure, though its sexiness is not as apparent to the modern eye as it would have been to a contemporary. She has taken off the plain beret she evidently wore with the outfit for the photograph and revealed that her hair is certainly not naturally corn-coloured as she, or her ghost, describes it in her memoirs.

dressmakers plenty of opportunity for display. The Society woman spent her morning in London writing letters and organising the business of her house: the PB was more likely to be seen in her riding habit before breakfast with the 'Liver Brigade', ridding themselves of hangovers by riding through the Park. After lunch a lady changed her tailor-made or quiet morning dress for something a little more showy, depending on whether she intended to shop or drive in the Park. The PB might pack a selection of showy outfits and spend the next few hours at the photographer's. For tea at 5 pm, the hour of most visits, both changed again, though they might ride in the Park instead. The pre-dinner hack through Hyde Park gave the crowds their chance to see the Prince of Wales riding with his latest lady.

A lady changed again for dinner, sometimes into a less formal dinner gown for an evening at home. The PB spent almost every night of the season in the low-cut, sumptuous, boned formal evening dress, for a programme of entertainments beginning with dinner, taking in the theatre perhaps, and concluding with a ball which could stretch from 10 till 5 in the morning – resilient health was among the many other qualities a good PB needed. Dinner was always in private houses, for restaurants were then places where no lady, beautiful or otherwise, might be seen to dine. In those decades affairs were conducted either at home in the afternoon (though there was always the difficulty of watchful servants), or very late at night, when an unmarked cab would be taken to the house of a third party, who had arranged for a latch-key to be handed over, the servants to have been given a brief holiday, and lobster and champagne to await the visitors. (Though the Prince of Wales regarded champagne as a common and clichéd drink, fit only for the demi-monde; Lillie was offered whisky or lemon and soda.)

There were special occasions throughout the season for the display of dresses. In May the private view at the RA gave the beauty a chance to exhibit herself near her portrait, where spectators could ponder the truth of *Woman's World*'s airy statement in 1888: 'The choice of a good portrayer is as difficult as that of a dressmaker or milliner.' On summer evenings there were drives through the country lanes of Fulham to Ranelagh or Hurlingham for polo, a band, strawberries and cream, for which Ascot-like dresses were worn if the weather was fine. There was Ascot itself in June, an excellent place to set fashions. Lillie scored a great success in her first season with a twisted black velvet toque, decorated by a feather, which she improvised herself – for Lillie, like Alexandra, could make her own clothes. In July there was boating on the rivers, in August Cowes. Then the rich went abroad or to Scotland, where the hostesses of the country houses who entertained the Prince of Wales's set ensured that droves of beauties would be present to amuse them. But by November the London-based had returned to the capital, where the PBs had time to think up new follies in clothes for the season ahead, and new extravagances of behaviour. For PBs set fashions in behaviour as well as in dress: when Lady Dudley drove in the Park with her small son sitting beside her, the beauties rushed to their nurseries to bring out the latest accessory and dress it to match. Beauties' fashions in behaviour were generally in the 'fast' category: they might smoke, for example, after dinner or, like Daisy Warwick, tear around in a four-in-hand.

11   The Regimental Ball of the Honourable Artillery Company in 1882 looks considerably more amusing than the State Ball at Buckingham Palace did in the previous decade (page 12). The illustrator is slipping in hints: a figure very like the Prince of Wales is dancing with a very fashionably-dressed and very young lady with a Langtry-style Grecian knot, while a stiffer, more bejewelled, choker-wearing figure in the background with a strong resemblance to Princess Alexandra chats resignedly to a handsome young officer. Lillie's affair with the Prince of Wales was long over by this date, but persisted still in rumour.

12 & 13   After the beginning of her stage career, Lillie was seen in the best of couture clothes on stage and in the magazines. Readers might copy from illustrations of the gowns for each new production which appeared, and compare them with reality in the flesh or with the photographed version. The Worth evening dress, drawn in the top left-hand of the illustration on the right, is shown in front view in the sexily-posed photograph above, complete with tiger skin, chaise-longue and velvet cushion. Those wearing corsets could not curl up invitingly, but had to remain rigidly skittle-like: no wonder that the tea-gown, worn without corsets, was so rapidly adopted for boudoir wear. Lillie's neck and arms were considered particularly firmly fleshed and attractive, which is why she has left them uncovered by jewellery.

40

Dresses worn by Mrs. Langtry in "Princess George" at the Prince's Theatre.

Made by Mons. Worth, Mons. Felix and Madame Doucet, Paris.

A combination of Lillie's fastness of behaviour and falling rents in Ireland, where the Langtry family held property, forced Lillie into a crisis in 1880. Mr Langtry was declared bankrupt (at the mere rumour of it, dressmakers' bills flooded in to Lillie) and she discovered herself to be pregnant by Prince Louis of Battenburg. To these circumstances can be attributed the second stage of Lillie's successful career as a Professional Beauty, this time on the stage. To support herself and her child, Lillie became in effect, a model – but not on a catwalk. Salon models were not to achieve glamour or wealth until the next century. Fine dresses had of course been seen on the stage long before Lillie's debut, but her success, unlike Sarah Bernhardt's, say, another beautifully-dressed actress, relied on dresses first and talent hardly at all. Though she worked at her acting, it was only ever a vehicle for the display of her face, figure and clothes. But that was enough. Those who had previously seen the photographs and heard the rumours were willing to pay good money to watch the lady, and her fashionable wardrobe, in the flesh.

Spurred on by the need for money, and also by a desire for some success which would compensate for the humiliation of her fall, Lillie

14 Bills from Worth were simply part of the necessary expenses in Lillie's business of self-promotion.

brought to the stage every scrap of professionalism she had learnt in Society. Where her fame had been exploited by dressmakers to their profit, Lillie began, in her new career, to exploit it for herself. She ran her own theatrical company, negotiated her own deals and collected the vast profits her face and dressing brought her. So great was her attraction that for her first visit to New York, in 1882, she was given the same terms for notoriety that Sarah Bernhardt had been granted for genius.

It was in many ways a repeat of her launch into Society. On her first New York visit even Oscar was there, on a lecture tour, and he was happy to repeat to reporters the bon mots and charming compliments about Lillie he had invented years ago for London use. Lillie handled journalists with the same ease and deceptive frankness of manner which had seduced the habitués of London's salons. She befriended New York theatre critics as she previously had the editor of the malicious *World*, and took the sting out of their reviews by doing so.

Her looks she regarded quite cynically as a bankable asset. She worked to keep them, watching her diet carefully and even, according to the New York *Sun* in 1886, jogging every morning for two miles to keep her figure trim. A highly active woman, she continued to ride – in breeches and shirt in California in 1887, astride her own horse on her own ranch. In life-style and in this dress she was about a half-century ahead of her time.

Much of her profits were re-invested in clothes. A huge wardrobe from Worth and other couturiers was necessary both for stage dress and for her off-stage publicity appearances. Any dress which seemed to suit her well would be ordered in several different colours. Worth himself thought her eye for cut and colour was so professional that she could have made a career as a dressmaker. With her staggering wardrobe and her legendary collection of jewels (some contributed by millionaire lovers and worth at one point £40,000 on contemporary valuation) she dazzled, taking real couture to the provinces of England and America as it had never been seen. Sketches of the dresses Lillie was to wear in a new production were given to fashion journalists and appeared in magazines. And though she refused to speak of her private affairs, rumours of scandal kept audiences interested in more than her wardrobe.

This publicity continued to be backed up by the trade in photographs which had already been under way when Lillie first appeared in London. Then it had been a very profitable business – for the photographer. The first pictures of Society beauties were taken in return for free prints for the sitter. The mere suggestion that husbands might be paid money for the wives' pictures to be sold or displayed was taken as an insult. When Lady Randolph Churchill's picture first appeared in the early 1870s in a shop window without her permission, her friends assumed that she would be furious. 'I was severely censured by my friends and told that I ought to prosecute the photographer,' she remembered, but soon after, publicity became the rage and a Society woman with any pretensions to looks felt humiliated if her picture was *not* on display, even though she collected no income from photographs.

Once turned actress, however, Lillie was able to tap the profits of the photographers. Actresses sold exclusive rights to take pictures to one photographer: Lillie sold hers 'for a very large sum' to the American, Napoleon Sarony, who also owned the right to photograph Bernhardt. The frequent sittings given under these contracts had some advantages for those who wished to imitate actresses' dresses. Since they were commonly photographed with each new play in several of the costumes worn in it, it was frequently possible for a woman who saw a dress on the stage which she particularly liked to buy a picture for her dress-maker to work from.

Fortunately for the beauty of the 1870s, the techniques of retouching improved as she aged. By the 1890s the sceptical photograph-collector looks first not to admire, but for the dark hollow by the waistline, the tell-tale mottling around the line of face and chin which indicates the removal of wrinkles, the whited-out dark circles beneath the eyes, and the traced-in line between the lips. On some of Sarah Bernhardt's later pictures her entire missing leg has been restored.

By the 1880s, new ways of using photographs of actresses began to emerge. Cigarette cards were introduced into America in the 1880s, and picture postcards were an instant success in Britain from their introduction in 1902. Cheaper than photographs, and more useful, they were collected in huge numbers. Pictures of women actresses and beauties were collected most often by young girls, who often scribbled comments on the clothes on the back of them as they sent them to other friends with collections. Something of the style, if not the actual dress, of an actress could be absorbed by studying postcards, and they were particularly good for close up views of hats and hair-styles.

There was yet another source of income for the PB turned professional which Lillie quickly tapped: the advertisement. Advertisements mentioning clients without fee had long existed in the press, sometimes with unfortunately frank details. Alexandra, for example, had the humiliation of seeing the firm of Unwin & Albert, in the 5 June 1880 edition of *Queen*, advertise themselves as 'Ornamental Hairdressers to HRH Princess of Wales' with details of her small arrangement of false hair, curled fringe at the front and knot at the back 'quickly producing the present fashionable coiffure' for the sum of fifteen shillings (75p). Lillie's name had been freely attached to Langtry shoes, Langtry dress-improvers, Langtry bonnets and so forth, to the benefit of those who made them; after her husband's bankruptcy, she herself sold it for profit to advertise products, to the horror of her former Society friends.

As a result of her wide and varied publicity and her appearances across the world, Lillie's influence was immense. This time it was not merely on girls who flocked to tie their hair in Grecian knots and copy her dresses. There were others who quickly saw that a beauty on stage could be a great commercial vehicle for promotion. America was ahead of the rest of the world in this respect: when Lillie arrived in New York, she was astounded by the offers of free clothes, hats and even meals in return for the publicity her name gave. Gritty businessmen were much influenced by Lillie's success and by her methods.

A range for stage beauties followed. The Gaiety Girls of the 1890s, for example, were chosen not for dramatic talents but for their looks and the ability to wear clothes with élan. Constance Collier remembered in her memoirs being taken on at the Gaiety at the age of fourteen. 'If I had been plain I should not have been engaged – the girls were not chosen so much for their ability to act and sing as they are nowadays . . . We only had to stand about in those days and nobody worried about a voice.' In this life pretty girls without much intelligence could easily find themselves jettisoned after a few cosseted years. But those who, like Collier, had ambition and determination, could use the start their looks gave them to further their career on the straight stage. Gladys Cooper was one who realised that the passion for good modern dresses had to be pandered to if she was to get on. A postcard beauty, she used some of the cash modelling gave her to buy better dresses than those she was given for minor roles on stage. In 1907 she was forbidden to wear one creation because Gertie Millar, the star, feared she would be upstaged. But by the time that Gladys appeared as Cecily Cardew in *The Importance of Being Earnest* at St James a few years later, she had learnt bold tactics. She chopped up her wardrobe dress with scissors on the first night and walked on in her own. The risk of losing her job was, she claimed, secondary to the risk of appearing a frump.

She was certainly right. By the 1890s British dressmakers and jewellers

15 Camille Clifford in 1907 in *The Belle of Mayfair*. The Gibson Girls and other popular actresses were given jewellery and dresses on loan for the sake of the promotion they gave to them, and their appeal on the stage was centred very much on what they wore. By the 1890s the latest developments in fashion could be as quickly discerned from a visit to the music hall or the theatre as to a Mayfair dress shop.

were so aware that stage beauties affected fashion that they too were lending out their goods for private appearances in restaurants as well as public appearances in the theatre. Reville was particularly generous. In borrowed clothes stage beauties might be seen, admired and copied, though it was all illusory sparkle. 'With the break of dawn a messenger would arrive to take my glorious raiment away and I was left like Cinderella in my rags,' remembered Constance Collier.

By the late 1880s there were as many dress critics as dramatic critics in the stalls. And by the 1890s high society, not merely those who rarely saw a couture dress, was finding inspiration behind the footlights. In the 6 January 1880 edition of the *World*, the fashion correspondent reported that many people were going to see the pantomime at Drury Lane in order to gain ideas for Drawing Room frocks. By gradual progression through the 1880s, the stage had become one of the most important media for the display of fashion, and dresses which appeared on it were reported in almost reverent detail in the magazines which catered for women. 'There has been . . . no important theatrical event since that important sartorial event took place – I refer, of course, to the introduction of the New Sleeve,' wrote *Queen*'s correspondent in the 22 February 1896 issue about a performance of *Jedbury, Junior* at Terry's Theatre. 'Miss Maud Millett was its wearer . . . sleeves of soft white silk, with a small damasked spot . . . they wrinkled, as Fashion's prophets told us they would, for most of the arm's length. But on the shoulders the silk became ebullient in the form of a couple of puffs, pushed up close together so as to resemble frills; at the wrist some creamy lace was

46

'folded around the sleeve, and was permitted to indulge in a fluttering end.'

It is impossible to imagine a similar description being written in the 1980s. Even the soap operas and costume dramas on television, which are dressed to attract female viewers, are not taken so seriously. But paradoxically the effect of such intensity of interest was to reduce the individuality of style of the actress in her dress. Managers and mantua-makers conferred to the maximum profit of both over what show of splendour would be most nicely calculated to bring in maximum audiences and sales. Anything novel or too innovatory would have been regarded as a foolish risk to a play's success by a manager in the 1890s and early years before the Great War. To be too far away from the mode could risk disappointing audiences who had come to expect a show of the very latest and richest fashion. But the Professional Beauty, once she was earning money from her looks, lost the originality of her amateurism and most of her freedom of choice in clothes – as did the Hollywood stars of the 1930s and the professional photographic models of the 1960s.

That was a sacrifice which Lillie willingly made. She preferred the stimulus of making money, doing business and learning to brilliant effect American methods of promotion. Indeed, so happy was she in that energetic and independent country that she took out American citizenship in 1887.

Since she had never been much impressed by her own looks, she was happy to sell them to audiences and a series of wealthy men, but she made sure she kept the profits. By the end of her stage career she was a dollar millionairess. Her old age was spent in luxury in the south of France, undisturbed by the knowledge that her face had disproved Oscar's youthful assertion that Mrs Langtry would always be a beauty. She allowed herself to run to fat, and she enjoyed her money. Which was a more stylish finish to a beauty's career than that of Mrs Patrick Campbell, who in old age and relative poverty demanded of Cecil Beaton and her maker, 'Why must I look like a burst paper bag? Why can't I be beautiful still?'

47

3
Dress for Dress's Sake

There could hardly be a bigger gap between the style and interests of the Society beauty (lady-like or professional) and the romantic. Unconventional, uninhibited in attire and certainly embarrassing for the average schoolboy to be seen with in public, women like Ellen Terry, Jane Morris and Sarah Bernhardt dressed for the sake of dress and of art. Each had very different styles, for individualism is part of the romantic's creed. But they had a common cause against convention and each, in her own way, was a few paces ahead of her time. Not only did they have a distinct and considerable effect on the dress of their day, but even a hundred years later traces of the romantics could be distinguished in the style of the fantasists and flower children of the 1960s and early 1970s.

The difference in their dress from that of Society women of their time was due to major differences of background. In the early 1870s Ellen Terry was as charming, natural and eye-engrossing as the Princess of Wales, but the highly irregular pattern of her life and dress formed a complete contrast. She made even the more innovatory beauties look conventional. She was not regularly pretty. Thick, curly and honey-coloured, her hair was her only obviously lovely feature. Her face was big-nosed and strongly boned. Her hands were large and capable, not the soft, small-fingered paws generally thought desirable for dependent Victorian kittens. Hard work looking after herself and her two children made her thin almost to gauntness – most unfashionable in the 1870s. But hers was one of those faces to which Lady Cynthia Asquith's description of the best of the beauties of her later day applies. Ellen was certainly a woman whose 'beauty is far more than an endowment; it is an achievement . . . their original loveliness is gradually enhanced by that flickering beauty of expression which delicate sensibility gives'. Her charm and beauty sprang from her character, from her swift, graceful, eager movements, the humour of her mouth, the direct, courageous gaze of her light eyes, her determined chin. In motion her face was alive with interest and delight. As a result she was 'to the

48

present prae-Raffaelites [sic] what Miss Herbert was to earlier members of the PRB – the cynosure and the divinity', as the theatre critic of the *World* noted in his review of her triumphant Portia of 1875.

A sarcastic description in the 12 May 1877 edition of *Punch*, summing up the type of the artistic woman, bears traces both of Lillie and of Ellen – both very influential on fashion at the time. 'A young lady with uncertain-coloured hair, short waist, long skirt, pale-grey eyes, a washed-out complexion, mulberry-tinged lips, and an arch expression about the bridge of the nose, who is the guardian angel of a second-hand furniture shop, not a hundred miles from Vinegar Yard, Drury Lane.' But Lillie was not of so humble a background as Ellen, born into a poor family of actors, and Lillie was too quickly adopted by conventional Society ever to wear aesthetic dress. Ellen, on the other hand, was separated from all conventional mores, even those of her own relations, by the accidents of her past.

In 1874, when she had returned to London to work as an actress again, her past, her career and her enforced self-reliance marked her out as a fore-runner of the new woman of the next century. She was intelligent, if uneducated, and determined. Her character had been early developed by her work in the theatre (one of the few places, as Florence Nightingale pointed out in her feminist tract, *Cassandra*, in 1859, where the mid-Victorian girl was allowed any serious training) and reinforced by personal tragedy in the shape of marriage. In 1864, a year after Alexandra's marriage, Ellen was travelling hopefully up the aisle to become, at the age of sixteen, child-wife and free model to the painter Watts, a good thirty years older: the marriage lasted just ten months.

Its more permanent effect was to introduce Ellen to artistic dress, which she was to wear in one form or another for the rest of her life. For though he was not a Pre-Raphaelite, Watts was influenced by their ideas on costume. Holman Hunt designed Ellen's wedding dress to incorporate several of the characteristics which would mark the aesthetic dress of middle-class Kensington fifteen years later. There was the muted colour – a shade of golden-brown which looked well with Ellen's dark golden hair – the elaborate sleeves, puffed and caught in, and, worn with it, the amber necklace which was to become to the aesthetic woman as the handshake to a Mason, a sign of membership of an exclusive band of the enlightened.

The end of Ellen's marriage removed her from the rich and beautiful surroundings she had been dressed to match, in the puff-sleeved,

16   A cabinet photograph of Ellen Terry dressed in the Whistlerian style. She sometimes wore kimonos like this in her private life in the early 1870s, while she lived with the aesthete Godwin, but her cheerfully independent stance belies any suggestion of the subservient geisha. Her large, capable hands were a feature she was ashamed of in her adolescence, but later she learnt to use them gracefully. This picture was probably taken in the mid to late 1880s.

17   Hardly in the expected image of the Victorian woman, Ellen Terry kept to a style which was frequently untidy and very often boyish. Girl admirers cut their hair short in imitation and tried to copy the striding walk and defiant poses. A cabinet photograph taken in 1881.

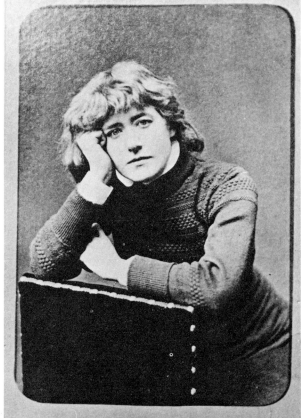

50

18   Alice Comyns Carr was thought by her friends to be the model for the gaunt, earnest figure of Mrs Cimabue Brown, seen here in a dress which combines the main features of the aesthetic movement: puffed sleeves, a natural waist, a Morris-type print and a general impression of drape and flow. The unconfined hair was another sign of the species. Miss Bilderbogie, like Alice, is about to marry for love, not money: sensible and suitable young men did not usually find that the artistic style of dress attracted them.

ÆSTHETIC LOVE IN A COTTAGE.

Miss Bilderbogie. "YES, DEAREST JOCONDA! I AM GOING TO MARRY YOUNG PETER PILCOX! WE SHALL BE VERY, *VERY* POOR! INDEED HOW WE ARE GOING TO *LIVE*, I CANNOT TELL!"

Mrs. Cimabue Brown. "OH, MY BEAUTIFUL MARIANA, HOW *NOBLE* OF YOU BOTH! NEVER MIND *HOW*, BUT *WHERE* ARE YOU GOING TO LIVE?"

Miss Bilderbogie. "OH, IN DEAR OLD KENSINGTON, I SUPPOSE—EVERYTHING IS SO CHEAP THERE, YOU KNOW!—PEACOCK FEATHERS ONLY A *PENNY A-PIECE!*"

short-waisted, crinolineless dresses which were the garb of the artist's wife. But it did not remove from her the appreciation and eye for beautiful objects and lovely clothes which she had just acquired. The next man in her life was even more fascinated by artistic dress than Watts: he was the aesthete and architect, E. W. Godwin, whose passion was for historical accuracy and all things Japanese. As a result, Ellen began a new Whistlerian phase in her dress, spending the years from 1868 as lover of Godwin and mother of his two children, wearing harmoniously-shaded mediaeval tabards and Japanese kimonos, without trace of fashionable bustle or padding.

She was utterly isolated from her contemporaries in circumstances as in dress. As a divorced woman, living in sin with her lover and illegitimate children, she was quite outside respectable Society. By 1875, when Godwin left her to marry a 21-year-old, she was entirely, and most unusually, independent. The cynosure of the Pre-Raphaelites, far from wilting in some ivy-laden garden, was striding around the streets of London in suitably boyish matador hats and swirling cloaks, from stage door to her own front door, earning a living for herself and her children on the stage.

But she continued to follow the aesthetic mode of dress, for aesthetic dress suited a free style of life far better than the rigid, whaleboned, pompously decorated dress of fashion. Its whole purpose was quite different. It was not intended, for instance, to please conventional men or to attract a good match. The garments of the romantic dresser had the reverse effect. In the late 1860s, when the artistic style of dress was just beginning to attract adherents who were not wives of artists and aesthetes, young Alice, dreamy, dark-haired daughter of the English chaplain at Genoa, spoilt her chances at a Tintern Abbey picnic by wearing a trailing robe and picture hat, an ensemble which was sniffed at by her elderly chaperone as 'theatrical'. The chaperone was right. Alice did not make a respectable alliance. Instead she married in December 1873 a poor drama critic called Joe Comyns Carr, and eked out the first years of her married life in two rooms in Bloomsbury, where the bed had to serve as a buffet table where they entertained.

She was a close friend of Ellen Terry's, and an imitator of artistic dress. Her high-waisted, straight wedding dress, its high neck trimmed with a frill, was similar to those being worn at the time by Jane Morris and Georgiana Burne-Jones. Tall, thin, with a large nose, hooded eyes and a shock of dark frizzy hair, Alice was a kind of aesthetic groupie, following others' lead with a simple, almost Boswellian earnestness. But she too influenced fashion. Respectable, and admitted into some parts of Society as Ellen, till the years of great fame, was not, she was a striking figure at all arty gatherings, and the model for George du Maurier's absurdly enthusiastic, drooping female disciple of the artistic movement, Mrs Cimabue Brown.

But if the strange dress of the romantics made conventional man of the period feel uneasy – the Prince of Wales disliked its untidiness – there was no doubt that it was, unlike the neat dress of the lady-like, deliberately sexy. Men who danced with aesthetic women soon discovered that dancing with the uncorseted was a quite different and more enjoyable experience than waltzing with whalebone. Going without corsets made life much pleasanter for the aesthetic woman, too, who made a point of wearing her waist its natural size and in its natural place. The most she might wear as support was a compromise adopted by Sarah Bernhardt, a little kid-leather vest. And the provocative absence of a corset, or indeed a petticoat, might be discernible to the eye as well as the fingers. Even the unconventional Vernon Lee, on visiting a Royal Academy private view in 1881, was startled to discover some most crazy-looking creatures; one wore crinkled gauze all tied close about her and visibly no under-clothing (and a gold laurel wreath).

The admired looks were sensual, too. Jane Morris's full lips live up to the description given by Thomas Hardy of another romantic heroine in art, Eustacia Vye: 'the mouth seemed formed less to speak than to

19   Dangerous to know, but alluring all the same, Sarah Bernhardt used dress to accentuate a sinuous sexiness which was entirely her own invention. Her thin figure was quite unfashionable, but she chose to exaggerate it by wearing waistless dresses with strong vertical trims. This costume, for her role as Mistress Clarkson in *L'Etrangère*, played at the Comédie-Française in 1876, contains all her characteristic touches: the high ruffles at the neck into which she drops her chin to allow a more compelling gaze, a flower by her face, a sensuous material – velvet – and the famous and tantalising front fastening. The long black gloves and fingered crop are hardly necessary to suggest that here is a woman of strong, probably uncontrollable, passions. Note the uncorseted slouch.

quiver, less to quiver than to kiss'. Jane Morris, corsetless, could curve invitingly on studio throne and chaise longue, but she was out-classed by the most sensual of all the romantics, Sarah Bernhardt, whose looks, like Eustacia's, gave an impression of mysterious and probably forbidden passions. The desire of Hardy's heroine, delivered to her public in 1879 at the height of the aesthetic craze, was 'to be loved to madness'. Bernhardt had a similar ambition, but it included her entire public. Her looks, dress and movements were carefully designed to seduce. Her lips, painted a deep, inviting red, were held slightly parted. Bernhardt outraged by painting her lips in public half a century before such conduct became acceptable. She was deliberately artificial, indeed her beauty, which depended on gesture, pose, and clever dressing, could be switched off and on. Brown eyes outlined with kohl mesmerised with druggy stare from their shadowed sockets. Her golden fluff of hair flamed about a powdered, pierrot-pale, face, her fingertips were painted pink and her ear-lobes were rouged.

She designed her dresses – they came from Parisian couturiers, but Sarah had her own ideas on how they should be made – to set off her face and emphasise her sinuousness. A double Pierrot ruffle cupped her flirtatious face, with a huge gauzy bow below to balance her strong profile, and some flame-coloured roses pinned to one side. The tight hems and vertical lines of her dresses exaggerated her slim figure and their front buttoning fastenings, from throat to hem, were as easily undone as the two pins which kept her curious hair-style of double tufts, like a rabbit's ears behind her head, in place. The dresses were made of supple silks or soft velvets, as pleasant to touch as to look at. And she glided invitingly across the stage like a snake rustling through autumn leaves, according to one hostile female observer. To all this she added a golden voice. 'I went,' she said, 'to extremes in everything.'

Sarah, like Ellen, had a less than respectable past, but by the time she first visited London in 1879, actresses of genius were admitted to Society whatever their morals. Used to the less liberal attitudes of Paris, Sarah was at first alarmed by the pile of invitations she received then from unknown aristocrats. In case there was any mistake, she took her illegitimate son along with her and had herself announced as 'Miss Sarah Bernhardt and child'. To her surprise, no-one cared. London Society women were far more interested in her clothes and her walk, and soon they too could be seen undulating freely up and down art galleries and drawing rooms in the Bernhardt way, with the Bernhardt tragic gaze. Artistic young ladies like Violet Lindsay copied her unkempt curly fringe.

For untidiness was another feature of the romantic dresser. While the fashionable lady pinned and prodded and padded her hair into a neat, controlled shape, the aesthete's hair was uncontrolled. Jane Morris's, crinkly and dark, was arranged for evening in great wavy projections on either side of her melancholy face. Ellen Terry's was a boyish mop of curls. Negligently worn hair had been a sign of the romantic since Byron and it had not changed much by 1932, when Stella Gibbon parodied the arty female in the figure of Elfine in *Cold Comfort Farm*, a girl given to 'brusque boyish movement', dull green hand-woven cloaks and unrequited love, whose 'unbrushed mane' and liking for poetry must be tamed before she could win the hand of the eligible Richard Hawk-Monitor.

The conventional lady was expected to keep her emotions, like her clothes, under control. The aesthete expected to display her moods in her dress: no stiff upper lip for her. It was a principle that Ellen Terry applied even to her stage dress, which she matched to the feelings of the character she played rather than the stage set, as Henry Irving discovered when he asked her what she had decided on for her performance as Ophelia in 1878 at the Lyceum. 'I told him . . . in the first scene I wear a pinkish dress. It is all rose-coloured with her. Her father and brother love her. The Prince loves her – and so she wears pink . . . In the last scene I wear a transparent black dress . . . I think red was the mourning colour of the period. But black seems to me right, like the character, like the situation.' What Ellen had overlooked was the colour of Irving's costume: appalled by the idea of a competitive black figure on stage distracting from his Hamlet, he ordered her to change her gown to white.

Ellen was notably disordered and moody in her dress, given to sudden enthusiasms inspired by memory or chance association. It was a recollection of past happiness which accounted for the eagerness with which, one hot summer's day in 1885, she commented on the cool, crinkled muslin frock Alice Comyns Carr was wearing. Rather to Alice's surprise, she instantly commissioned one just like it for her next stage part, and began a partnership with Alice as stage dress designer which was to last many years and be highly influential on fashion. But the real reason for Ellen's delight in the dress was that one very like it, a simple tie and dry affair, had been the first dress Godwin had designed for her when, a mere child before even her marriage to Watts, she had played Titania in his home town. It had been the first lovely frock, she said, that she had ever had.

She was so anxious to preserve past associations in her costumes that she advocated a kind of sartorial anti-scrape policy. As William Morris cherished the patina of old buildings, so Ellen Terry valued the patina of old frocks. In her old age she told Sybil Thorndike, 'Never have clothes cleaned for the theatre. It takes all the bloom off. The dirt has got something in it which you'll miss if you send it to the cleaners.'

For the aesthete, there was a strong connection between buildings and dress. The same aesthetic principles governed both, and dress was carefully chosen to complement surroundings. While Alexandra could happily wear her strictly-cut suits to write her morning letters in a boudoir crammed with sentimental treasures, the aesthetic woman of the time found her nerves jarred if the wallpaper clashed with her skirt. As a result she had to dress very carefully when going out. In the rooms of her friends there were only two types of decor which she might expect to encounter, the Rossetti-rich, or the Whistler-white. In the rooms of Philistines it was impossible to predict what horrors might be encountered: die-hards called in advance of a party to check the colours of the walls. Ellen, in her Godwin years, dressed to match a Whistler type of background: bare wooden or matting floors, cool painted walls in pale yellow, grey or white, a few plain rugs, little furniture, a lot of blue and white porcelain. A kimono fitted perfectly into these surroundings, as did a dull green gown, or a soft grey. Whistler once matched his own decor for an exhibition by wearing yellow socks, and Constance Wilde (Oscar was another follower of Whistlerian interior decor) wore white and yellow stockings.

If Whistler's style of decoration was all simplicity and light, the Rossetti style was cluttered antique gloom. Coloured light filtered through stained glass windows or massed plants, and tapestries absorbed much of even that poor illumination. In these kinds of houses dresses in a rich antique style, in deep colours and lush materials looked best. Fancy sleeves and deep folds, as worn by Jane Morris, were ideal. She chose dead purples and deep blues, which looked well against the embroidered hangings and polished wooden floors of Kelmscott.

Sarah Bernhardt, typically, designed her decor to match herself, turning her studio into a stage set for a sorceress and a seductress, with yards of draped velvet and dim light. Portraits of herself stared down at the heaped cushions and her canopied day-bed, upon which this modern Circe might arrange her serpentine curves. Skulls, stuffed vultures and a coffin added to the dramatic effect.

Rooms and interiors were important to the aesthetic dresser, for aesthetes were essentially town-based. The country did have a romantic attraction, though: Ellen Terry spent nights awake on her lawn in Sussex, gazing at the moon, and amazed her village neighbours in Winchelsea in later years by dancing at dawn in her garden in a flimsy nightgown. Sarah Bernhardt went shooting, gallantly attired in breeches. But their approach was very different from the robust, sensible, solidly-based familiarity with country matters and large estates which the well-bred lady displayed in her tweed Norfolk jackets and Abergeldie hats, worn for an afternoon's fishing or walking.

It was knowledge of another kind which the aesthete displayed in her dress, an academic familiarity with the history of dress, or an artistic appreciation of line and tone. At its best it was charming, at its worst it showed an intellectual snobbery just as calculating as some of display of wealth in fashionable dress. Some of the most beautiful results of the academic approach to dress were worn by Ellen Terry in the 1875 production of *The Merchant of Venice*, gowns designed by Godwin to match the period of Venetian history so accurately that many of the

56

details were not seen beyond the stage, gowns which made the aesthetic audience gasp: a honey and cream embossed velvet, a dress like cherry blossom, scarlet lawyerly robes. They were to usher in a period of historical accuracy in stage dress which lasted through until Beerbohm Tree's productions in the 1890s and 1900s.

20   In 1876 the Olivia cap made almost as great a sensation as the Langtry bonnet, and versions of Ellen Terry's headgear from her part in *The Vicar of Wakefield* at the Royal Court appeared in milliners' windows all round the country. Contemporary fashions of the time had a strong eighteenth-century flavour.

Even historical dresses like these had their influence on fashion. The puffs of Ellen's sleeves and the colour combinations of her dresses were imitated by arty young misses who came to watch her act. She provided constant inspiration for costumes for the fancy dress balls and fêtes so popular from the 1870s through until the end of the century. The lace cap she wore as Olivia in *The Vicar of Wakefield* in 1878 became the rage: those who missed her performance saw the 'Olivia bonnet' in the thousands of cabinet photographs produced of her in the part. Perhaps most influential of all was a dress with fine, blue silk, accordion-pleated skirt, now in the Museum of London, designed by Ellen Terry and Alice Comyns Carr and made by Mrs Nettleship, dressmaker wife of a minor animal painter. Worn by Ellen in the part of Margaret in *Faust*, produced in 1888, it created a mania for fine pleating. Its impact can only be understood in terms of the productions of *Faust* seen in England and the States: almost all Henry Irving's productions toured in America (Ellen calculated that she spent five years of her life there in all) and *Faust*, a triumph of design as well as acting, was particularly popular. There were 128 performances in America, 577 at the Lyceum in London and 87 in the British provinces. By the late 1880s Ellen Terry's face was so well known that she could not go out into the streets without being mobbed. And she had complete control over her own stage costume in her Lyceum productions with Irving, as no actress would today. Her contributions to fashion, though informed by her education in Watts's and Godwin's hands, were largely her own.

Ellen's historical dress was chosen solely because of its beauty and appropriateness to a part. There was no pretentiousness about her. But an academic approach to historical dress at its most charmless was exemplified by Mrs Haweis, middle-class (and social-climbing) wife of a fashionable preacher. While the Reverend Hugh pompously instructed middle-class women on their souls, his wife tackled the subject of their costumes. Author and fashion journalist, she was a useful interpreter of the fashions more creative women had worn: she helped bring the aesthetic mode to the masses.

She was a minor artist's daughter who had had a girlish admiration for Rossetti and picked up on some of his interest in mediaeval dress. She attentively noted old costumes in portraits in art galleries at home and on trips with her husband abroad. The information was neatly stitched into fashion articles which gave her status and more work: eventually she became the most notable fashion journalist in England since Mrs Beeton, twenty years before. The competition was not stiff, but Mrs Haweis could write well and knew a lot about her subject, and she spread her knowledge to the middle classes through articles and to Society in person. And since she had a mind of her own ('it is no part of the milliner's business to think for us', she wrote) she had sufficient confidence to review the dress of London Society as of some interest on its own merit, not as a reflection of the glories of Paris. For, like Oscar Wilde, she believed that contemporary fashion, as well as historical dress, was 'a tendency worth study and eminently instructive'. It was an entirely new idea to the readers of her fashion books and of her columns in *Queen*, where she wrote from 1878.

Though her dress was very far from being Pre-Raphaelite or Japanese in inspiration, it was quite distinctly historical. Since she was small and plain, with a great desire for attention, she decided that rich dress of the Carolean period suited her best. Not only her surroundings but her son was dressed to match: he, luckless boy, was put into the costume of the court of Charles II, and her house in Cheyne Walk, once Rossetti's, was filled with Carolean furniture, including a heavily-carved four-poster bed. Mrs Haweis's clothes were not simply Carolean: she was more ambitious than that. From descriptions which survive it seems that they were a strange mixture of historical, modern, and arty elements. Though she was given to standing around at parties tut-tutting over the historical inaccuracies in other people's dress, her own was quite bizarre. At the second Drawing Room of the 1880 season, for example, according to *Queen*, she wore a dress she had designed herself, trimmed with a collection of antique laces and a jumble of aesthetic flowers. 'Mrs Haweis wore a petticoat of elaborate Italian design, in which a peculiar red, blue and gold were the prevailing colours, trimmed with broad Venetian point lace; train of prune plush, trimmed with Venetian point, wallflowers scattered *au naturel*, and a single large sunflower in one corner; ornaments, diamonds and antique brown amber necklace, buttercups and white plumes in the hair and old point lappets.'

It seems to have been fairly typical of her individualism. On a visit to Lord and Lady Mount Temple at their Palladian mansion, Broadlands, in 1872, she decorated herself with acorns in lieu of jewels. No wonder that when she died in 1897 the *Times* obituary declared, 'She was thought peculiar and so she was.' None the less, she induced many of the aristocracy to accept her pronouncements on taste, her crowning achievement coming in 1880, when Princess Alexandra adopted her economical new fashion of 'prepared seaweed' as a trimming for ballgowns. Red, white or green, mounted on wire, this decorative vegetable could also be worn as sprays for the hair.

Inverted snobbery about jewels was one of Mrs Haweis's specialities. She herself admitted that she wore necklaces of beads chiefly because she could not afford diamonds (those she wore for her Drawing Room appearance were borrowed.) It is true that the cheapness of the aesthetic mode helped to popularise it amongst the arty, but less prosperous, middle classes. As Mrs Haweis advised, in *The Art of Dress*, published in 1879, 'There are many ways of saving in dress. One is not following the fashion, but adopting the style of some period to be studied from pictures, which is soon seen to be a "fad" of yours, and people get tired of making fun of you if you hold out, having right on your side.' But though aesthetic dress was soon picked up by the aesthetic groupies of South Kensington as a cheap way to be fashionable, its original intention was to disdain the show of wealth in fashionable dress.

Unlike the dress of the lady of the period, or the beauty, the romantic's dress was not designed to show wealth or rank, her husband's or her own. Quite the reverse. She wore sprigged cotton of a kind worn by servants. Ellen Terry remembered an incident from her youthful days in Hertfordshire as Godwin's mistress when she displayed a disregard for class which shocked her servant. 'I went to church in blue-and-white cotton, with my servant in silk. "I don't half like it," she said. "They'll take you for the cook and me for the lady."' Aesthetes abjured the bustles, crinolines and long trains which lowly servants also, because of their work, had to go without – though even the lowliest prided herself on some silk or fashionable feature for Sunday best. Cotton dresses were not acceptable social wear for those in the Alexandra rank of life until the 1950s, when Princess Marina was known for her Horrocks' frocks.

Morris did not convert to socialism until the early 1880s, and the subject bored Jane. But there are early features in her aesthetic dress which point towards Fabianism. The simple lines of Jane's dresses in the 1860s look more like those of women labouring in the fields and on the beaches than those of her contemporaries. Later smocking, the decorative pleating and stitching which had enlivened the masculine overall of the agricultural worker since the early nineteenth century, was taken as a motif for the dress of high-minded middle-class women. Ellen favoured it from the mid-1870s to the mid-1880s: photographs show her in soft dresses of silk or wool, smocked at the head of the sleeves and near the cuff, at the waistline or at the yoke, giving an unsophisticated bloused effect quite different from the tight, straitjacket line of conventional dress in that period.

Nor did the aesthete's clothes demonstrate their wearer's wealth by their large number. It was not necessary to have many artistic garments. They did not go quickly out of date because they were never intended to

21 & 22 (above)   Two artistic families pose for the camera in 1874, Jane Morris (front row) looking mournfully at the ground as she had for many a Rossetti sketch. Her day dress barely changed throughout her life, as a comparison with the (retouched) photograph of her in old age demonstrates (left). The high-necked dress with its slight ruffle, high waist, gathered sleeves and slim skirt remains much the same, even to the detail of the smocking which gathers the sleeves at the wrists. So does the hair-style. Georgina Burne-Jones, on the extreme left of the group photograph, wears a dress with elaborately puffed sleeves, very similar to those in which Ellen Terry was sketched by Watts ten years earlier. With the Pre-Raphaelite revival of the early 1970s came similarly arty gowns: the dress Jenny Morris (next to Georgina) is wearing could have been sold in Laura Ashley in 1974.

61

be of their time, as Mrs Haweis had observed. Mrs Newbery, wife of the headmaster of Glasgow College of Art, wore a Carpaccio evening dress from 1889 till 1904, when she discarded it out of pity for local Society journalists who had run out of ways of describing it. Jane Morris can be seen in photographs still to be wearing similar dress in old age to that which she wore in her youth. For not only was the kind of frivolous fashion change, also shunned by the lady-like dresser, avoided, but so were the modest seasonal changes in shape and colour which the lady-like watched so carefully. 'And after all, what is a fashion?' loftily enquired Oscar Wilde in an editorial for *Woman's World* in 1887. 'From the artistic point of view it is usually a form of ugliness so intolerable that we have to alter it every six months.' The aesthete, on the other hand, need not alter hers in so many years.

Diamonds, those brilliant markers of wealth and position, the favourite jewels of Alexandra and her friends, were anathema to the Victorian romantic. Sarah Bernhardt loathed their cold, souless glare. 'I have a horror of sad jewels, of sombre stones,' she said. 'Jewels ought to be happy . . . I detest diamonds.' She, like Ellen Terry, chose jewellery to match her hair, not her income. Burnt topaz (she owned a live

23   Sarah was not disconcerted by rumours that she was a transvestite boy, and liked to wear her own version of a pierrot suit for work in her studio. Even then she kept the rules of her personal style of dress, choosing to have a jacket made with a long line and retaining the ruff and gauzy bow. The half-up, half-down hair-style was held in place by two pins only, but this principle of easy naturalness was not extended to her face which, even with a boyish suit, was carefully made up.

tortoise set with topazes) and gold set with pearls (she married in an old
gold gown with gold and pearl jewellery) were favourites. So was
turquoise, a stone familiar to British aesthetes from the paintings of
Alma-Tadema. Amber and strange beads were the favourites of Jane
and Ellen.

The savings the aesthetic woman made were not only in money but
also in time. Loose and simple gowns, like those Jane and Ellen wore,
were easy to put on and take off. Those who, like Alice Comyns Carr,
could not afford a maid, found the business of dressing in artistic dress
simpler, and some of the endless turning and re-making of garments
the conventional genteel classes of the 1870s were put to was spared
them. It was a straightforward style of dress, and it was well suited to
lives of women who worked as actresses or writers (Alice wrote, as well
as designing dress for the stage). It suggested the direction fashion
might take when there were fewer cheap woman-hours available to
spend on clothes, and when more women had serious work to occupy
them.

There were other indications of the future in the romantic style. Ellen
Terry's cropped hair cut was one, and was imitated by some of the girl
fans who flocked to see her, for she was an actress with a strong female
following among the girls who were now coming out of the Oxbridge
women's Halls.

Sarah Bernhardt's trousers were another signpost to the next century.
If it is hard to imagine how rebellious the act of cutting short a 'woman's
glory' seemed to the church-going Victorians, it is almost impossible to
understand how sinful Sarah's pretty, frilled pierrot suit was thought.
The overtones of transvestitism only amused her. She wore trousers to
sculpt in because she found them easier to work in, but it would be
unwise to deduce from this that she was a supporter of rational dress.
No word could be more foreign to Bernhardt; indeed, the sober maidens
who advocated hygienic dress reform were scathing about Sarah and
her butterfly appearance. Ellen Terry, with her fisherman's sweaters
and easy stride, made her a far more likely heroine for those who fought
for women's rights.

The advantage of freedom of movement and cheapness of price
attracted many free-thinking women in fields other than the theatre and
the arts to wear aesthetic apparel: Elizabeth Garrett Anderson, for
example, who had a high art house, and whose skills Mrs Haweis had
procured for her confinement in 1870.

So innovative, in fact, were the romantics that the garments they

24   An ageing Sarah Bernhardt in 1895, still gallant in breeches, this time out shooting in South America. The dropped mediaeval waistline was another of her favourite looks and was particularly useful as she grew older and fatter. But Bernhardt's notion of masculine dress was not hailed by supporters of rational costume, who found Bernhardt far too effeminate and picturesque for their tastes.

wore had by the 1880s had a direct influence on even the most philistine wardrobe. But it took a little time for the ideas of this group to ripple out from their small beginnings. In the 1870s their ideas were confined to a small band of like-minded friends prepared to be thought very odd by the rest of the world. Informal meetings and parties, like the picnics in Alice Comyns Carr's Bloomsbury flat and breakfast at Whistler's, gatherings in studios and backstage drawing rooms provided opportunities for the women of group to influence only each other.

Like the dress of modern art students, their strange costumes deliberately defied prevailing standards. The mockery received only made them knit more closely together in dress and mannerisms. The exclusive nature of the group attracted the curious – and the artistically-minded avant-garde amongst the aristocracy. By the mid-1870s imitators could be seen in Society circles, though few. By 1877, when the Grosvenor Gallery opened, owned by Sir Coutts Lindsay, with Joe Comyns Carr as one of its directors, the pretentious, poetry-loving women caricatured in *Punch* are beginning to wear a recognisable dress: free-falling, often printed and puffed-sleeved. Since in the 1870s and 1880s there was still very little visual information in magazines on what real women, as opposed to fashion-plate models, were wearing, *Punch*, and particularly du Maurier's excellent detailed drawings of dress, was one of the best sources of ideas around. As early as 1862 a writer was lamenting in the *Englishwoman's Domestic Magazine* that caricatures of crinolines in *Punch* intended to put young women off them were simply being used to copy from. Du Maurier's drawings, which showed the aesthetes growing ever more droopy and oddly-gowned as the beginnings of the 1880s drew nearer, so successfully spread knowledge of this English cult to America that when Ellen Terry appeared there as Ophelia in 1883, the critics found their enjoyment of her performance spoilt by a ludicrous resemblance between her gestures and those of du Maurier's poseurs.

By then the romantic style of dress was very well established as a fashion in Society and amongst some of the middle classes. The Prince and Princess of Wales attended receptions in the Grosvenor Gallery, where good examples of admired artistic dress were prominently displayed on the walls. It was particularly useful for women commissioning portraits, since it was thought less likely to date than contemporary fashion. By 1880 it had made its appearance on aristocratic backs in the very highest of Society's functions; in that year, for example, the Countess of Dunraven wore a Pre-Raphaelite dress of a dull red shade with a high bodice and large puffed sleeves to a Drawing Room. It was not so different from the wedding dress Ellen had worn sixteen years before. And by 1880, Ellen herself, not just her dress, was accepted into Society. The barriers against actresses, who at the beginning of the decade had been classed as tradesmen and only admitted into private houses to perform, had fallen. The dress and mannerisms of Terry and Bernhardt might influence Society direct. The middle classes had, besides *Punch*, Mrs Haweis's keen eye to help them appreciate the aesthetic mode, and cabinet photographs of aesthetic actresses were popular.

There were other, stranger routes of influence open to the aesthete forbidden to a lady. Trade, for example. Ellen Terry's association with Arthur Liberty may well have developed from a meeting in the house of her sister, Kate, who had married a partner in the silk mercers, Lewis & Allenby, and kept an artistic open house to visitors like Millais and Leighton. The ambitious Liberty opened his shop in the year of Ellen's successful Portia, and from then on she bought many of the materials for stage and private dresses from him. So close were the links between Liberty and her friends that when he began a dress department it was

THÉÂTRE DE LA RENAISSANCE

LYSIANE

Mme SARAH BERNHARDT

Godwin he put in charge of the designs for it – designs which, for the most part, had already appeared earlier on Ellen. They were the very garments Liberty had been meeting her in for years. And there were further inter-connections: another of Liberty's acquaintances was Mrs Haweis, to whom he lent materials in return for free promotion.

The middle-class woman who shopped at Liberty might study Ellen's dresses on the stage, and those Parisian interpretations of the romantic mode worn by Sarah Bernhardt. Sarah's dresses, usually contemporary though always with the mark of her personal style upon them, were the most copyable. They also had the most professional finish, and they were far more professionally marketed than Ellen's. She, like Lillie, pre-released drawings to the magazines, along with written descriptions of the changes for each act. For *Frou-Frou*, for example, she wore in the second act 'a tea gown of white and coffee-coloured lace with a high ruche and pale yellow roses near the throat'. And, as Lillie did, she stimulated yet more interest in her dresses by her extravagance. Those women who went to watch Sarah could be sure of seeing their money's worth in clothes: for her 1880 tour of the USA she spent 61,000 francs on thirty-nine costumes, employed two full-time lady's maids and travelled with more than forty trunks full of costumes and baubles.

Those who preferred the simple, Athenian mode of costume, as worn in the 1870s by servants at Leighton's studio house, might see it in the less exclusive setting of the Lyceum in 1884, worn by the American actress, Mary Anderson. Her performances in *Romeo and Juliet* and her highly popular photographs popularised the crimped or pleated robes she wore, held together by buttons at intervals along the upper arms and casually tied across the bosom. If she finally brought the Athenian gown, which so influenced Fortuny twenty years later, to the attention of the middle classes, it fell to Mrs Bernard Beere in the mid-1880s to popularise the most influential of all the dresses of the aesthetic movement – the tea gown.

25 Ladies' magazines were, by the '80s and '90s, giving full illustrations of the costumes important actresses chose to wear. Bernhardt adapted to changes of fashion (this was for a production at the Lyric in 1898) without losing the stamp of her personality. Soft clinging dresses, with pouched low waists or none at all, long lines and a high ruff still spell out Bernhardt. Although couturier-made (as her dresses always were), it is quite a different look from the stiff, jaunty Gibson-Girl style (see page 46).

26   Mary Anderson, the American actress who popularised Grecian dress in the 1880s by wearing it on and off stage. Worn without a corset, with tumbling hair and apparently insecure fastenings, its sexual allure was straightforward. This version appears to be made in cotton crepon or a similar fabric. It remained popular as a stage dress at least until 1914, and Isadora Duncan wore something like it in private life as well as for stage exhibitions of dancing.

The tea gown was eventually worn in the most determinedly philistine households in the land: more than that, it summed up all the most important qualities that the wearers of romantic garments valued. It was loose, it was easy to put on and off. It was sensual – indeed, it later became the classic garment for the seduction scene, being easy to slide in and out of without having to call for a maid, and being made of soft, tactile materials. In it, it was possible to breathe easily and curve naturally: corsets were not worn with it until the late '80s, when the middle classes began to wear it generally and try to make it 'respectable'. It was extremely useful wear for the pregnant. And this easy, lounging gown was usually made with some pretty historical features, like a Medici collar, or puffed sleeves, or a sack-back. Even in the 1890s they were made in 'aesthetic' gentle colours – salmons and greys, yellows, soft greens, shades of rust and cinnamon. They fell in an unbroken line from throat to waist in soft folds. Over the gown was worn a contrasting open 'coat' or, later, a tea jacket, to preserve decency and hide a little of the figure which the soft draperies revealed.

The tea gown held many of the characteristics which were to become commonplace in day dress in the next century. It stands in relation to the aesthete as the classic suit does to Princess Alexandra. And in 1887 Oscar Wilde perceptively noted the essential similarity between these two apparently very different garments, when he wrote in *Woman's World*, in a review of the current fashionable's wardrobe: 'With the exception of M. Felix's charming tea gown, and a few English tailor-made costumes, there is not a single form of really fashionable dress that can be worn without a certain amount of absolute misery to the wearer.'

The beginnings of this humane dress can be traced as far back as the beginnings of the artistic style of dress, though it did not exist under that name in the 1860s. The style of it was in the air, however. Wally Paget claimed in her autobiography to have picked up the coming style by designing of a loose, high-necked dress with a front inset of a different colour quite by accident in about 1866 when staying in Scotland: 'I evolved the first tea gown out of my inner consciousness and wore it at Cluny and other places where there was a small party. It was in black satin, opening in the front of pale blue satin and the sleeves were of the same colour. It was trimmed with old guipure lace and I wore a little cap of the same. The ladies all hailed the innovation. . . .'

Well they might. For the tea gown, in the true, liberated spirit of Terry, did not expose the chest and arms to cold Scottish draughts or to the gaze of the curious, and it did not bone the waist so tightly that it was difficult to eat a decent meal. Unsurprisingly, the tea gown was swiftly adopted in feminine circles, for the feminine rite of 5 o'clock tea in the boudoir, where tea gowns – at first loose aesthetic gowns of any kind, and even kimonos, which tea gowns often drew inspiration from – looked well against a background of straw fans and blue and white china.

By the 1870s the tea gown was beginning to be known. By 1878 it was mentioned in the press, though even a decade later it was new enough in the wardrobes of the middle classes for the women's magazines to need to explain that it was not worn as outdoor wear and never with a hat. What it did do, however, was move down from the boudoir to the dining room. The advantages of comfort made it an excellent garment to dine in informally at home.

Once the ease of the tea gown had been felt, it could not be long before the rest of the wardrobe began to relax its whalebone grip on the female figure. Ellen Terry's soft, woollen dresses with their smocking at neck and waist had had their insidious influence: so had Sarah Bernhardt's flowing, corsetless dresses in which she had swathed herself across a thousand stage chaises longues.

The influence of the romantics, as serpentine as Bernhardt, has twisted its way in and out of the course of fashion ever since. Just when it seemed totally dead at the beginning of the twentieth century, Isadora Duncan appeared in her Greek draperies, Fortuny revived the Athenian gown, and the art of smocking re-awoke once more. A little over half a century later, Jane Morris's picture was to be seen on every university campus, and latter-day Pre-Raphaelites sulked on the covers of *Vogue*.

Even in 1982, Lady Diana Cooper was to be seen at parties wearing a coral-pink, tightly-pleated gown by Yuki, derived from Fortuny, inspired originally by the aesthetic dresses her own mother, Grosvenor Gallery stunner Violet Lindsay, had worn a century before. The dress which *Punch* had ridiculed upon the back of poor Mrs Cimabue Brown, alias Alice Comyns Carr, for its nostalgia for the past had proved itself triumphantly to be the dress of the future.

4
Beautiful and Wise

By the last decade of the century, Society seemed to have changed remarkably little. The Prince of Wales, in late middle age, was still playing the undignified part of a feckless youth, and the names in the gossip columns of the women who dominated the party round of the season were surprisingly often identical to those who had led it in the 1860s and 1870s. Princess Alexandra was still the acknowledged leader of the lady-like, still receiving endless compliments on her long-surviving beauty, though her dress had fossilised a lttle in the mode of the 1880s. The Duchess of Manchester, now the Duchess of Devonshire and hideously ugly, was still powerful enough for her approval to be necessary for any beauty who wished to succeed in Society. Around the Prince and his ageing roué friends clustered much the same lively group of women whose photographs had filled the shops ten years before – though Lillie Langtry was absent. And though the middle classes had adopted paper fans and sunflower motifs so enthusiastically that the aesthetic movement was now quite passé, the aristocratic 'stunners' who had once drooped prettily in the Grosvenor Gallery were now part of a new group of high-minded 'Souls', with a distinct manner of dress which retained many of the romantic features of the aesthetic period.

In all categories, however, there were important changes, and not just in the faces of the well-known beauties. All felt the influence of the coming century. Old shibboleths died hard, but already women were beginning to have more freedom of choice, more independence. There were signs of it in their dress.

It was most marked in the dress of the women who were members of the Souls, the small, well-born, unofficial intellectual elite of Society. Unlike Ellen Terry and Sarah Bernhardt, they had been born into the upper reaches of the upper classes, with all their unwritten laws of dress and behaviour. Clever and talented, they had no need to work at anything, and no need to upset convention. Many of them were amateur artists and amateur writers nevertheless, and they took from the professional artists and actresses they mixed with some of their habits of dress and behaviour. Their clothes revealed a romanticism which had been a little diluted by worldliness.

It was very clear in the dress of Violet Lindsay, one of the loveliest and most copied of the Souls. A girl with abundant, marmalade-coloured hair, tragic eyes and a Pre-Raphaelite profile, she had been one of the sensations of aesthetic circles in the early 1880s. Because of her good birth she had married exceptionally well, despite her penchant for a romantic mode of dress, to the Duke of Rutland's heir. As Marchioness of Granby, and a talented artist and sculptress who knew the leading figures in Bohemian circles in her time, she bridged two worlds.

She admired Princess Alexandra with schoolgirl enthusiasm. But she also admired and imitated her friend, Ellen Terry. Her dress showed both influences in the late 1880s when the Souls began to be known: it was distinctly arty, but with a trimness and distinction which was a little more formal than the full romantic mode. Her dresses were a little high-waisted, as the Pre-Raphaelites recommended, but they were very slim at the waist, worn with a high head and a straight back. She avoided high-fashion changes (the extremes of the 1890s puffed sleeves for example) but there was always some link with contemporary fashion in her clothes. She was horrified by the idea of spending vast quantities of money on 'fashionable dress' and she trimmed her own hats with a confident hand – but she obeyed Society's rules on the correct times for the wearing of gloves and hats.

Like the rest of the Souls, she was careless of some conventions. Throughout her long affair with Lord Hartington, the Duchess of Manchester had strictly obeyed Society's rules and never once addressed him in public by anything other than his title. In the avant-garde circles of the Souls in the 1890s women called men, whether friends or lovers, by their Christian names or even, a shocked Lady Paget noted, by the disrespectful title 'Dear Man'. Violet Granby was equally high-handed with the Rutland heirlooms: an artist out for the effect which best displayed her particular looks, not the family jewellery, she wore the Rutland tiara on the back of her head and her earrings to keep her scarves in place. Her hair, once shockingly cropped in the Ellen Terry manner, was worn in the 1890s in an unruly golden fringe after the style of Sarah Bernhardt. In the evenings she might throw a diamond-sprinkled net over her top-knot. Nor did her dresses display wealth: they were pinned together by her or run up to her imaginative instructions by a small dressmaker, often in the creamy

colours and rust shades which suited her red-gold hair. She had nothing
by Worth. Her own label, her particular hallmark, was old lace, dripping
from throat and sleeves, tied Bernhardt-style in bows by her face,
pinned with more diamonds over the holes, and with the bay leaf
which was the membership badge of the Souls.

When the Duchess of Devonshire threw her famous fancy dress ball
on 2 July 1897, and hundreds of pounds were lavished on elaborate
costumes by the women invited, Violet Granby typically avoided all
sordid competition and spent not a penny. More than that, she avoided
the ludicrous by simply choosing to go as a more extreme version of
herself. In an ingenious assortment of old laces, draperies and
diamonds, with a lace net over her hair, she claimed to be imitating a
portrait of an earlier Duchess of Rutland, and looked – as usual –
beautiful and at ease while less intelligent women stumbled over their
farthingales and sweated beneath brocades.

The whole effect of Violet Granby's dress was artistic. It was certainly
charming. But it was just as certainly not what Society expected from a
Marchioness. Because she was an artist talented enough to exhibit, she

27   The Marchioness of Ripon, a
'stunner' of the late '70s and a patron of
the arts, famous for her arrogant
expression and haughty beauty. An
aesthetic dresser, she is here seen in a
tea dress, in what looks like an Indian
print.

28 The Soulful look at its most romantic. Violet Granby prepared for the Duchess of Devonshire's fancy dress ball by digging around in the dressing-up box at home and putting a lot of pieces of old lace and oddments of material together in what is merely an exaggeration of her usual look. The Bernhardt influence on her tawny hair is apparent: she wore a similar fringe, though she once chopped off her curls in an effort to resemble Ellen Terry, a close friend. The eccentrically-scattered jewels are worn with as much aplomb as the hole torn in her lace hair-net.

had her own independent status, and she dressed for herself. By doing so she helped to break down a little of the stuffiness surrounding women of rank.

The dress of the female members of the Souls was not intentionally rebellious: there was nothing strident about it. Their intellectualism was not of the kind which despised fine dresses or pleasant surroundings or sought to change the structure of Society. Like Jane Austen, they were perfectly at ease in their time and, like Austen, deeply interested in dress. Burne-Jones's painting of the Countess of Plymouth in 1893 shows something of their intensely feminine style: the fluted folds of soft material, the highish, very narrow waist, the draped neckline, downcast eyes and languorous pose of body. 'In my day,' said Mrs Patrick Campbell, an intimate of the Souls women and much admired by them, 'beauties moved and spoke very slowly, giving the impression that they had just been possessed.' There was nothing boyish about them, but there was nothing sluttish either. The morals of the Souls

74

29 Millicent, Duchess of Sutherland, at 25. A great beauty and a half-sister of Daisy Warwick's (it was a family of beauties), she regretted the fact that her eyes lacked the dreamy softness necessary to an artistic style. But she had a taste for simple dresses and for holding lilies in her hand as she welcomed guests to balls in Sutherland House. Fashion and her own looks were an obsession.

were no more stern than those of the circle which surrounded the Prince of Wales, but sexual adventurousness was not signalled in their clothes. If there was a sweet disorder in their dress it never bordered on the slovenly. As for cosmetics, they were regarded as improper: Violet contented herself with a beauty routine which consisted of washing her face in soft sterilised water, powdering with fuller's earth and rubbing a little pink lip-salve on her mouth.

It would be wrong to suppose that the Souls were less snobbish than their contemporaries. Instead they added intellectual arrogance to the pride of rank. The simple bay leaf was a mark of a very exclusive band. 'Common' was Violet Granby's favourite term of reproof, and all kinds of manners of dress were dismissed under that heading. The antique lace she wore might and did have holes in it, but it was valuable and yellowed. White lace was 'common'. So were bright colours (though favoured by Lady Desborough, another, less choosy member of the set). Faded blues, greys and greens, as approved by Godwin and Burne-Jones, were acceptable. At a time when Ellen Terry was laughing at the pretentious way she had dismissed other people's dress in her early years, the Souls were still proclaiming their superiority of style.

There was a hint of the future in the relative plainness of their dress, but it was only a slight one. The Duchess of Sutherland, a great beauty on the extreme fringes of the Souls, whose lovely, heart-shaped face looked best in the simple white and black draped dresses she stood in, lily in hand, at the top of the staircase in Sutherland House to receive her guests, went to the Duchess of Devonshire's sumptuous ball as the revolutionary figure, Charlotte Corday, in plain red dress and mob cap – but the dress was silk.

Quiet, refined and graceful, the dress of the Souls women followed many of the precepts of Beau Brummell dandyism. It avoided excesses and was always subordinate to the wearer, so that the admirer looked first at the face and not at the trimmings. It was much more attractive and becoming than the heavily-loaded fashion contemporaries were wearing in the 1890s. But because it was removed from high fashion, it necessarily had lttle influence outside Society. The dress of the Souls was barely reported in the fashion magazines, though this aesthetic set did influence the clothing of other women in the peer group because it was so prestigious. They were even said to have set a trend for reading amongst ladies of leisure. And of course they strongly influenced one another. The most remarkable example of that process was Mrs Harry Cust, who turned herself into a look-alike of Violet Granby, in similarly draped laces, identical hair-style, even similar poses, in the hope of capturing the heart of her own husband, who was not only in love with the beautiful Marchioness but the probable father of her youngest child, Lady Diana Manners. It was a hopeless business. The copied version only reminded Harry Cust more strongly of the original, and his wife went to her grave – draped in lace to the end – knowing that she had lost the fight.

Far less appealing in dress, but far more influential outside their own circles because they were in the mainstream of fashion, were the beauties of the previous decade who had now dominated shop windows and the gossip columns for more years than most of them cared to contemplate. The Prince of Wales was a loyal, if sentimental friend. He liked the company of these women, who knew what chatter of scandal and politics would best entertain him. But the beauties were now a more experienced and more obviously determined bunch than they had been in the light-hearted 1880s, and their frocks reflected their strong characters. Most notable amongst them was Daisy Brooke, later to be Countess of Warwick, risen from being a fresh young girl in a white debutante frock sprinkled with innocent daisies to being mistress-in-chief of the Prince of Wales. Her independence in dress sprang from an independence of income, for Daisy was an heiress and

30 & 31   Two Souls with but a single thought: the former Miss Welby (right), wife of Harry Cust, and Violet Granby (below), who was for years his mistress and who is believed to have born him a child – Lady Diana Manners, as blonde and beautiful as he. In one of the strangest examples of fashion influence, Mrs Harry Cust closely followed Violet's style of dress, but she was disappointed in her hope that she could attract him back from Violet.

These photographs, taken in about 1891 by Cyril Flower, Lord Battersea, at Aston Clinton, show typical Souls dress: a cross between the romantic and the conventional, with its casually draped scarves and laces, but tightly pulled-in waistline.

no-one, least of all her husband, presumed to control her actions or her dress. She represented only herself. A beauty as well as an heiress, she had limitless confidence, and her fortune and her birth put her on a far more equal footing with the Prince than Lillie had enjoyed in her youth. Not wise, except in a worldly sense, Daisy impressed by her forcefulness. She drove her own four-in-hand, hunted incessantly and pursued the men she wanted without a trace of coyness or discretion.

Daisy's confidence showed in her stance and her dress. There was no doubt that Daisy looked her masterful best in mannish tweeds and habits, standing slouched in front of her own house with her hands deep in her pockets – a defiant gesture in itself – and a tight, bright-eyed smile on her face. Her country wear was wholly functional, and it was obvious that it was. In country house photographs, while other women look uncomfortable in heavy outdoor clothes, Daisy, chin to the camera, relaxes in her Norfolk jacket and thick-soled boots as cheerfully as though she had just returned from a tramp through her own estates, dogs at heel. Her happiest days were spent at Tattersalls, eyeing horse-flesh and being eyed herself, or in the hunting field where she set fashions in habits, though she rode only side-saddle – even the independent Daisy did not take to trousers, though riding astride was common in America by the end of the century, nor to going hatless, though again, in advanced America, girls could be seen playing tennis bare-headed in the hope of bleaching their hair as early as in the mid-1880s.

It was a pity that Daisy did not set a lead in rational dress, for the promoters of bifurcated garments were beginning to lose heart in the mid 1890s. No amount of lecturing or article-writing appeared to have much effect on the public. But, as the *Lady's World* remarked in 1887, a lead from the top of society might have done the trick. 'If Lady Haberton' (President of the Rational Dress Association) 'will get a becoming rational dress and persuade a few dozen pretty and stylish-looking women of high position to wear it daily in the parks during the height of the season, she will do far more to advance the objects which she has in view than by lecturing to an audience of ladies.'

Out of the fields and Rotten Row, Daisy's influence followed a curious course. For while her sporting style was much admired generally, her taste in evening dress was followed outside Society and jeered at in it. In drawing rooms and ballrooms, and even at race meetings, her dress was showy in the extreme. Red velvet was a favourite, despite her red hair, and the more elaborate a toilette, the better she was pleased. From 1890, when her liaison with the Prince began, Daisy received more mentions in the gossip columns than she had even as a beautiful unmarried heiress, and her dress was described in careful detail. The worldly *World*, by the '90s a paper of tittle-tattle rather than serious comment, described her appearance with a malice which can have been missed by few of the inner circle. It is a series of sartorial outrages. 'Positively dazzling in grass-green with a crimson sash' was Daisy at Newmarket in 1891. At the second Drawing Room of 1892 she appeared before an angry Princess Alexandra wearing imperial purple. At the opera she was to be seen in 'Mephistophelian scarlet velvet' with 'her exquisite hair' caught up in a narrow scarlet net. Her dresses, even in day time, were littered with diamonds. Eventually even the *World*'s correspondent, seeing her series of hints ignored, tried the direct approach. 'Lady Brooke has the most poetic instincts as regards her clothes,' she began flatteringly, 'but sometimes makes mistakes. Tea gowns and tea jacket in bright scarlet or green velvet with yellow or violet sashes, however effective they may be at night, look almost vulgar at the breakfast table.'

But while the upper classes were warned, the less sophisticated, middle-class *Queen* magazine was willing to recommend Daisy to its readership with only a suspicion of sarcasm which, if intended at all, would not have been picked up by the majority of women. 'You may generally take it as a certainty,' ran an item on 4 January 1896, 'that any firm where the Countess of Warwick deals is up to date, a remark which particularly applies to Mme Frederic, 17, Lower Grosvenor Place, SW. Of late she has been honoured by many orders from her ladyship, the garments in every case being singularly novel.'

The dichotomy between Daisy's influence on the women of her own class and women outside it was made all the greater by the fact that by the 1890s the magazines and newspapers had a far greater demand for women of fashion they could 'market' to their readers – especially those involved with the Prince of Wales. Fashion magazines and papers vastly increased in number at the end of the century and the slow process of engravings had at last been outmoded: photographs could now be reproduced, somewhat smudgily, in magazines. There was by now a constant coverage of the dresses of leaders of fashion in words and some photographs, with sketches given by court dressmakers to supplement the descriptions. Even the stuffy *Illustrated London News*, which had run barely more than a line or two on the dress of wedding guests in its issues of forty years before, now had a fashion column which gave its readers thorough descriptions of the latest mode. The middle class was well informed and so, at last, were the rest. Twenty years before, the *News of the World* had contained nothing of Society's doings save the occasional murder or scandalous divorce case. In the 1890s, however, came the growth of the popular illustrated press, with proprietors well aware of the value to their advertising departments of a strong female readership. By 1903 an entire paper aimed mainly at women of the lower and middle classes had been launched, the *Daily Mirror*, plentifully illustrated with sketches of fashion and studio photographs of beauties. It carried a whole page on the dress at the wedding of Daisy's daughter at Warwick Castle, for example, with illustrations.

The quality of reportage had grown correspondingly more sophisticated. Now there existed in England, as there had for a long time in Paris, a species of female journalist which specialised in attracting invitations to Society events and giving picturesque accounts of the dress of those who attended them. By the 1890s such journalism was an acceptable occupation for even the best-connected women. Lady Angela Forbes, Daisy's half-sister, edited the woman's page of the *Daily Graphic* for a while. It was a useful additional means of income for those increasing numbers of women who were, like Lady Angela Forbes, divorced.

The professional fashion journalists regarded their work with pride. The best were invited to the small parties women held to show their court dress to their friends before Drawing Room presentations. They had the connections to infiltrate balls and receptions. Unable to take notes in public, they had to bear all the details of Daisy's latest toilette, and a dozen others, in their heads: they had to recognise the leaders of Society and be in touch with the latest gossip. But according to one such journalist, who described her work in the April 1890 edition of *Woman's World*, such publicity was by no means unwelcome to the women described. They would spread out their trains before her like an ostentation of peacocks, in the hope of reaching the Society columns, much in the way that a stream of hopefuls had visited the photographers' studios in the late 1870s thinking that their picture might be prominently displayed beside that of the noted beauties. 'If you consult the wearers it pleases them,' noted the fashion correspondent with professional condescension, 'but they will always tell you wrong: and have some complicated name for a colour.'

There was no need for complicated names so far as Daisy was con-

32 & 33   Close acquaintances and
rivals, both as determined as they were
dashing, both recognised beauties, both
firmly in the Prince of Wales's fast
set: Lady Randolph Churchill (above),
dark-haired and very amusing
company, looked at her best in strict
riding habit, as here, or in dramatic
evening dress. It was her green-blue,
beetle-wing-decorated dress which
inspired Ellen Terry to have her Lady
Macbeth dress, painted by Sargent,
sewn with beetles' wings for a rich,
Rossettian effect. Daisy, Countess of
Warwick, and mistress of the Prince of
Wales from 1890 (below), also looked
her best in country tweeds and riding
habit, but in the evening she wore
over-ornate dresses which clashed with
her flaming hair. Both were admired and
copied, and both loved clothes.

cerned, and she was fortunate in other respects in her chosen colour, for the 1890s were a fashionable period for the scarlet woman. The Duchess of Manchester in the 1860s had been a strong-willed, highly experienced woman in an age when innocent, flower-bedecked young things had been the rage. The influence of the circle of beauties around the Prince of Wales had made the fashionable age grow with them. By the 1890s the vamp and the characterful woman were in fashion. Ladies with a past were all the rage. Lady Randolph Churchill was one of them, very much in the Prince of Wales's set, a shop-window beauty of the 1870s whose lively conversation and gay spirit were as well-known as her strong-featured face and the dark hair which were best set off by the simplicity of a riding habit. She was another masterful woman, whose qualities were seen as distinctively American and (most persuasive to imitators) ones which attracted the Prince of Wales. 'There is life and blood in her and love of fun; nor has all sincerity been crushed out of her by over-civilisation,' snootily noted the *World* in March 1892.

The compliant, butterfly, mischievous mistress of the 1880s had moved on to become, if possible, even more mischievous, but a good deal less compliant. She wore high-fashion dresses of elaborate cut, fine jewellery to mark her many successes, a degree of artifice about the face and hair and she was cynically witty. Firmly in this category was Lady Colin Campbell, rejoicing in the maiden name of Blood, an Irish beauty whose divorce from her husband made her turn to her pen for amusement and income. Art critic of the *World*, she wore her dark hair up and curled on her forehead to set off a mocking smile and dark eyes to best advantage. She was particularly fond of a sinister combination of black and emerald, perhaps in view of her Irish blood. Scarlet and black was an equally popular colour combination amongst mature '90s beauties, and that was what Jennie Churchill chose for the opening night of *Lady Windermere's Fan* – a black dress and a ruby velvet cloak with a deep cream lace frill. On stage Marion Terry (another friend of the Prince of Wales) as Mrs Erlynne showed that the woman of scandalous past was as entertaining in fiction as in fact. Wicked and witty, she delivered her succession of worldly-wise lines in a succession of seductive gowns and cloaks and obviously hennaed hair, parted in the middle and curled on her forehead. Such was the popularity of the type that a craze for hennaed hair followed the success of Wilde's play.

A series of popular plays in the 1890s portrayed the woman of scandalous past in parts which called for much fluttering of figure-revealing tea gowns. It was in one of these, Pinero's *The Second Mrs*

34 Stella, Mrs Patrick Campbell, was an idol of the female Souls, with her striking, gypsy-ish looks and a dangerous reputation. Vamps were expected to dress in sumptuous clothes and to look mysterious and experienced. Stella lived up to her looks by removing Lady Randolph Churchill's young second husband from her clutches and marrying him herself.

Tanqueray, first produced in 1892, that Mrs Patrick Campbell suddenly came to fame. Her photographs flooded the shops and she was instantly lionised in Society as the scarlet woman par excellence: everyone hoped that her real life might have been as mysterious and tragic as the stage part she played.

Her looks certainly helped to give that impression. It was on them and not her talent that she was cast, according to the artist, Graham Robertson, who remembered in his autobiography, 'She did not look wicked. She was almost painfully thin, with great eyes and slow, haunting utterance; she was not exactly beautiful, but intensely interesting and arresting.'

With natural intelligence, and a past interest in aesthetic dress, it was almost inevitable that Stella Campbell would become a friend of the Souls as well as the more philistine circles of Society. She claimed to be irritated by the assumption that she must be a woman of questionable morals, but if she was not when she took the part of Mrs Tanqueray, then she was a plain case of nature imitating art. She was rapidly to become known as a woman of wit, with a gift for the startling sentence, and by the time the new century was under way she was involved in a real Society scandal twice as entertaining as anything on the stage: filching from her dear friend Jennie Churchill her youthful second husband. For the beauties who had, in the 1880s, known older men with a taste for being amused by pretty young women, were in their own middle age developing a taste for being amused by handsome youths. Lillie Langtry married one; Jennie actually married the son of Lillie's old friend Mary Cornwallis-West. It was all splendid gossip, and fodder for the popular papers. The Professional Beauty had moved on a long way from her original passive role.

Even the circles of the lady-like had received an infusion of independent spirit by the 1890s. It was also being portrayed on the stages of the West End: the young American girl, beautiful, puritan, but with ideas and money of her own. The type was to have a considerable influence in Europe chiefly because, as Lady Caroline Pontefract sourly remarked in *A Woman of No Importance*, first produced in 1893, 'These American girls carry off all the good matches.'

Their success was not entirely owing to the wealth they could bring to the enfeebled estates of the Old Country. American girls were fresh, lively, better-informed and more interesting company than the majority of upper-class English misses. Wealthy American girls were properly educated – in sharp contrast to upper-class British maidens, whose education was horribly neglected, despite the advances being made in the late nineteenth century in upper-middle-class education for women. It was clear that in America the progress towards independence of mind and of dress was taking place far more quickly than in any other country. Large numbers of middle-class American women were in employment in the cities by the 1890s, and similarity of pursuits, as Oscar Wilde had prophesied, had led to similarity of dress. The girl from the New World had a distinctive style of dress, one which was mannish and crisp, based on the tailor-made and worn with a 'shirt', a tie, often as not, and in summer a boater. She did not fit in with the Old World's idea of the subservient wife.

Most famous and most influential of the American women who married into the British aristocracy and discovered the chasm between the old manners and the new was Consuelo Vanderbilt, who became the Duchess of Marlborough. Well educated and highly intelligent – she would have preferred to have gone to one of the new Oxford

35 A highly intelligent and sensitive woman, Consuelo Vanderbilt was trapped in the 1890s in a household which clung to the ideas of a woman's place being that of a status symbol and jewellery display stand which had been current in the 1860s. She evolved a fragile Dresden beauty of her own which was admirably suited to Edwardian chiffons but not so well matched by the elaborate and heavy velvets and furs which her husband, the Duke of Marlborough, preferred to see her in. This sketch is by a sympathetic friend, Lady Granby, later Duchess of Rutland.

women's Halls than Blenheim Palace – she was amazed at the ignorance of the English girls of her own age she met, and at the worldliness of the smart crowd her husband mixed in.

Introduced to the milieu of Professional Beauties, the Riviera, in the winter of 1895 by her young husband, she reacted just as Hester Worsley, American heroine of *A Woman of No Importance*, might have done: 'How different was this life from the prim monastic existence my mother had enforced. The goddess Minerva no longer sat enthroned. Beauty rather than wisdom appeared to be everyone's business.' But the beautiful young Duchess was equally dismayed by the goddess the Marlboroughs worshipped: propriety. It was unfortunate for her that her mother had picked on Marlborough as a suitable mate. His family was particularly pompous, and the code of behaviour they subscribed to had moved on not a whit from the 1860s. The girl who was fabulously wealthy in her own right discovered that she was not expected to have control over the type of clothes she wore: they were intended to display her husband's importance, though they were bought with her own money. On her honeymoon, as she indignantly recorded in her autobiography, her husband and Worth together decided on rich, over-elaborate clothes which drowned her delicate looks: a blue satin evening dress trimmed down the length of its train with ostrich feathers; a deep pink velvet gown with sables; a sable-lined coat to warm the Marlborough pride. Her jewels were not heirlooms – they too came from the Vanderbilt coffers – but her sister-in-law presumed to tell her when she should wear them: it would be a blow to the family honour, she was told, if she appeared in the evening without her nineteen-row choker of pearls encircling her long neck.

It was not likely that Consuelo would simply succumb to the Blenheim pomposity. Gradually, as her confidence in herself and her contempt for her small husband grew, she developed a style of dress which was indisputably lady-like, but less rigid, more delicate, and altogether more suited to her fragile beauty. It was in some ways a compromise between the old laws which covered the gentlewoman's dress and the new independence in the air.

One of Daisy's young half-sisters, Lady Angela Forbes, saw Consuelo in the June after her marriage, at Ascot, and was surprised by the change in her looks which had already taken place since her honeymoon. 'She had a great success, and looked quite un-American with that very small refined head on that very long neck,' she recorded.

On her wedding day, Consuelo, who was to become one of the most noted fashion leaders of her day, had had only the promise of beauty. Her features were small and, in profile, rather like a marmoset's. Not only was her natural elegance hidden in her over-decorated clothes, but she was unfashionably thin and tall – at five feet ten inches she was tactlessly taller than the Duke himself. So lacking was she in curves that it was reported that she wore her famous pearls, when not round her neck, in a horsehair pouch over her behind.

Bored and unhappy, Consuelo used her intelligence in one of the few areas where she was allowed to exercise it – in dressing. She exploited her defects. Her clothes were simplified to accentuate her height and reveal her long throat with the tiny head, worn tilted, drawing all eyes. Her high, arched eyebrows held a permanent expression of childish surprise. With her dark hair heaped on top of her head, a pale face and a small, pursed mouth, she looked like a Japanese etching. Violet Granby became a friend of hers and was among the many artists to sketch that refined little face. She was a natural ally of Souls women, but she did not adopt a Soulish style of dress. Her fashions were markedly contemporary, but of very delicate, pretty materials – floating chiffons, pale pastels, tinted laces. The Dresden Shepherdess air she had, in her wide hats, gave Edwardian fashions a charm they lost on more robust beauties. In the summer of 1902, for example, Consuelo was at a bazaar in aid of French charities at the French embassy, in a typical outfit noted by the *Illustrated London News* correspondent, looking 'graceful in a gown of silk muslin striped fawn pink. The bodice was fully pouched, the lower half of both the bodice and the big sleeves being of lace. A shoulder cape of net with brown spots, and a Leghorn hat trimmed with cherries, apples and pink apple blossom, completed the costume.'

Consuelo was fond of eighteenth-century costume: with powdered hair and a patch she was the sensation of fancy dress balls. In it, and in contemporary afternoon and evening dress, she looked her best. The pouched waistlines of the Edwardian period, the abundant materials and the shaped corsets gave her bean-pole figure a pleasing shape. In slimmer country tweeds and in the straight clothes of the 1920s she was far less fetching. But it was not the case that all Consuelo's attraction sprang from her clothes, for much of her charm came from her natural poise. She never sat: she perched. Her long, slender-fingered hands were always gracefully employed. Her back was held straight, her head pulled up to its highest extent then slightly tilted – she never made the classic mistake of tall women by slouching in an attempt to disguise inches.

With her air of distinction, her beauty and her lovely clothes Consuelo lived up perfectly to her rank. She was the fairy-tale Duchess: those who waited by the steps of Mayfair mansions to see aristocrats go in dressed for the ball were not disappointed in her looks. Possessing a fortune, she spent rather more money in the Paris couture salons than a lady was generally able to, but there was never any hint of vulgarity (apart from those first Worth honeymoon garments) about her wardrobe; it was supremely lady-like. Nevertheless, she dressed for herself and for her own sense of beauty. Her independence was finally demonstrated the next century when she separated from her husband and lived in Society on her own terms: she continued to be received, continued to lead fashion and preserved her reputation, and she continued to be breathlessly followed by the fashion press. For Consuelo was a gift to Society columns on both sides of the Atlantic from the moment her engagement to one of England's most famous Dukes was announced in 1895. Fascinating to readers were the intimate details of her trousseau revealed in *Vogue* right down to the decoration on her silken drawers: her signature, embroidered on the left knee.

Vogue, the new fashion magazine, published first in America in December 1892, took a deep interest in the wardrobes of all fashionable Society women. The editor and owners well understood that a mixture of straight fashion reporting on the Paris couture houses and the glamorous doings of their customers was essential to bring their subject to life. Most glamorous of all of the women whose portraits they ran full-page, and whom they showed at Society events through the year, were American heiresses like Consuelo who had married high British titles, combining the Old World and the New. It was also editorially useful, since *Vogue* soon began to sell in Britain, and the transatlantic fashion element was enlarged. The magazine was consolidating the two-way influence which had already existed since the 1880s.

One of the travellers in that traffic was the highly lady-like Mary Leiter, as beautiful and as intelligent and characterful, if not as rich, as Consuelo Vanderbilt. Her looks were more typically American than Consuelo's; Mary possessed the wide-eyed face, with its strong eyebrows and determined chin, still to be seen personifying the American look on the covers of *Vogue* in 1980. Indeed, Mary Leiter was, in her way, a model. She was drawn by Charles Dana Gibson in the boyishly alluring dress of the young American woman: the wide skirt which had become popular because by the 1890s more sports were being played by women, the stiff-collared shirt and the jaunty tie, worn with an abundance of hair parted in the middle and piled on top of the head. And she had the characteristics of the new woman: she was intelligent, clever, socially competent and extremely resilient.

Mary Leiter should have typified to London Society the dress and manners of her own country, but she did not. For, like Consuelo, she married a man whose approach to women and to fashion was based on the old, conservative, unwritten rules as to what was proper and dutiful. Consuelo was horrified, when she met Mary in her first years in London, by her subservience, for Mary changed her entire style of dress and looks to please her husband: took her hair down from its modern style to the more womanly, more gentle style of the '80s, as Curzon thought it, with the knot at the back of the head and the waves curving by the side of the face. It did not suit her personality or her face so well. Photographs reveal that the neat sailor-collared blouses and serge skirts of her girlhood were replaced in early married life by the kind of

88

drooping, lacy clothes popular amongst the Souls women with whom Curzon had mixed for years.

But what Consuelo did not understand was the important difference between Mary's marriage and her own. It was, in Mary's case, a willing and deliberate submission of style to please a husband whom she deeply loved and whom she had freely married. She was anxious to dress to delight her husband. She was more than willing to display his rank in her gowns. Unfortunately, in the first years of her married life, from 1895, she was hardly able even to exercise her intelligence in that restricted sphere. Her social life barely existed. But when in 1898 George Curzon was appointed Viceroy of India, her energies were more than well employed in the small sphere of activity which George Curzon felt was proper for a woman. Her wardrobe, overnight, became second in importance only to Alexandra's. She took her position as Vicereine as an enormous compliment to herself and to her country of origin, and she took to the business of organising her wardrobe with all the enthusiasm of an intelligent woman who has been without occupation for years.

It was not a particularly easy task. Curzon, more than most Viceroys, felt that it was essential to show the power of his place in symbolic magnificence as well as in action, since this was a concept the Indians expected. Mary had to dress splendidly, but there was comparatively little money to work with. Her father had just lost much of his wealth and Curzon was not, by the standards of his class, rich. Hard bargaining with Worth, in which Mary displayed some of the strengths of character with which she served her husband, resulted in a considerable reduction on her total bill for her initial wardrobe. At the end of her first two years she was able to write in trumph to her parents that her costs 'for two whole years, and you know I get every bit from Worth, is only 5,500 dollars, and that includes all my state dresses and every bit of my Indian array'. Few women, she added, came to India in her position with as modest a wardrobe. Or, she might have justly claimed, as successful a one.

For Mary perfectly understood the necessity for theatrical effect, for dresses which would look well from long distances at her public appearances and at the huge balls and receptions she had to attend. Her triumph was to achieve an appearance of magnificence without offending the tastes of the English society in India by appearing vulgar. She did it by using clear colours, which looked well in bright sunshine and against the kaleidoscope backgrounds of India, and by choosing

36 A spontaneous and charming smile was the least of Mary Curzon's many virtues of appearance and of personality. Richly dressed for India in order to announce the dignities of her husband's position as Viceroy, she contrived a splendid wardrobe with the help of Worth, her own imagination and skilful native embroiderers and dressmakers. Born Mary Leiter, an American heiress, she was one of the originals for Charles Dana Gibson's sketches of the liberated, starched-smart, new American woman, but she willingly changed her appearance to meet her husband's preference for a more submissive-looking, lacy, feminine appearance. Here she leaves the Viceregal Lodge at Simla for a drive in 1903.

elaborate trimmings of lace and beautiful embroidered fabrics, many of which, fortunately for her purse, could be commissioned on the spot. Even in England, where lavish hand-embroidery was the sign of an expensive ball dress in the Edwardian period, it was common practice to have material shipped out to India, embroidered and shipped back in order to save money. Not only was the process a great deal cheaper for Mary, on the spot, but she could direct the local craftsmen to create exactly the designs she wanted.

Since she was tall – five feet eight inches – and very slim (her waist measured less than twenty-six inches in 1903), elaborate designs did not overpower her, and her pale face, dark hair and strong features looks well against the bright colours she picked. In 1903 she wrote to her parents in typically lively style of the kind of dress she was able to have made: 'I had a most lovely Empire dress made here of Benares stuff – with a wide gold border, made over sky-blue crepe de chine, little train from the shoulders, absolutely upstanding lace collar and long wing-like floating sleeves. George said that he hoped I had a decent sort of frock and I told him I would work up something. He was amazed when I burst upon his astonished gaze in my celestial garment and he could only ejaculate "Gosh!" '

90

37 Alexandra, now Queen, and a jewelled icon – though some of the gems she is wearing may be paste, for which she had a fondness. Her face is heavily retouched to remove the lines, and her front hair is false, but she retains her slim waist and that confidence of pose which riveted attention wherever she went.

Curzon's reaction summed up the general opinion of Mary's success as Vicereine. She was greatly loved and much admired. So much, in the event, was she respected amongst her peers that the leader of the lady-like herself demanded her advice and expertise. In May 1901 Queen Alexandra asked Mary to deal with the making and designing of her Coronation dress and three others, intended for Drawing Rooms and balls in the weeks leading up to the event, and told Mary that she would leave the work entirely in her hands. She could scarcely have found a woman with a more practical understanding of the job the dress had to do. Mary took to her task with the kind of seriousness her husband devoted to his duties. One of the grandest occasions when she had studied Alexandra's style was at the Duchess of Devonshire's

91

fancy dress ball, when Alexandra, as Queen Marguerite de Valois, had worn a splendid costume with a high Medici collar, covered in paste stones and fake pearls to show off her slender neck and her jewels.

Mary's design for the Coronation bore some similarities to the dress for that other fancy dress occasion. It was a bronze-golden gauzy-looking gown with long winged sleeves and the Medici collar, a perfect foil to all the Coronation jewellery and regalia. Mary spared herself no work to ensure that the designs for the Queen and similar dresses for her mother and sisters, which she ordered at the same time, would be correct. 'I have had them all on the floor,' she wrote, 'and traced the designs through marking paper till my back nearly cracked.' All were made in mourning colours.

Besides appearing beautiful they were, as Alexandra preferred, very thriftily produced. Despite the uniqueness of the occasion Alexandra's bill was tiny: they ranged from £30 to £60, the average price for an average Drawing Room dress, at a time when a Court dress could cost over £300. And they had the advantage, since they were commissioned in the Empire, of appearing patriotic. The provenance of the dresses was well-known. The *Illustrated London News* informed its readers on 21 June 1902 that, at the last court of the Coronation year, 'Her Majesty had set the gracious example of employing the natives of India in the preparation of the Court dress that she wore on this occasion. Lady Curzon, at the Queen's request, has ordered several dresses for Her Majesty to be embroidered in India, and the one worn upon this occasion was an example. It was of the finest net, richly worked in many colours, gold thread predominating. It was worn over mauve satin, and was accompanied by an Indian necklace, and ornaments of rubies and emeralds.'

Alas, Alexandra threw away the advantages of her patriotic gesture. In independent mood, now that her mother-in-law was gone, she sent her Coronation frock to Eugénie's old fashion capital, Paris, and to Morin Blossier, her couturier, whose label remains within the garment at the Museum of London, though it seems likely that he only carried out final fittings and adjustments. This was despite the expressed wish of Alexandra that ladies' Coronation robes should be of English manufacture. If her ladies felt incensed and outclassed, English fashion journalists were equally furious, for Morin Blossier, insensitive to protocol, scooped them by releasing details and sketches of the dress to the French press before it had even appeared on Her Majesty.

It was a rebellious action on Alexandra's part, or a piece of

38 The famous peacock dress worn at the Delhi Durbar in 1903, made by Worth. Of good material, with jewels sewn into each eye, it managed to be at once magnificent, graceful and quite unlike Queen Alexandra's golden Coronation dress.

mischievous one-upmanship which Mary Curzon would never have allowed herself. When Mary's turn came to commission a magnificent dress for the Coronation Durbar in 1903 it was a triumph of tact, suitability and theatricality. It was so different from Alexandra's that there was no question of competition. Designed to be worn in a room lit by electricity, its skirt was made of shining gold and silver Indian embroidery, which shone with jewels in every feather. The rich material was cut by Worth into a supremely simple style, with a wide skirt and tight bodice. Not least of the tributes to Mary's charm was the fact that the peacock emblem was understood by all to be a symbolic statement of the pomp of princes, and not her own vanity.

But even the demanding Queen Victoria had realised, when she arranged a meeting with Mary Curzon to decide whether an American could possibly be a suitable Vicereine, that she was an unusual woman. Beautiful and good she evidently was. Victoria, contemptuous of vanity, saw something more. Mary Leiter, in her thoughtful opinion, was a rarer combination: beautiful and wise.

5

Bohemia, True and Blue

Lady Diana Cooper remembers that her father seemed to be always worried about money during her childhood. By the 1900s most aristocratic families save the filthy rich were beginning to find it difficult to maintain their standard of living and some were even resorting to filthy means just to stay ahead of the money-lenders. By the summer of 1914, for example, Daisy Warwick had run through her fortune and had thought of the clever idea of indirectly blackmailing King George V over his father's love letters in order to keep the cash flowing.

But all was sweet, demure order in the fashionable dress of the Edwardian period: chiffons of pastel hues were draped with lace and the adorable tea-rose face of Lily Elsie was the innocent type of loveliness admired. Yet even in the garden party and the ballroom there were signs of decline. Susan, Lady Tweedsmuir, recalls gowns being re-made with fresh pieces of tulle and lace patched on to cover stains and rips. Long gloves for balls, remembers Lady Diana Cooper, were rarely new so frequently grubby, or reeking of cleaning fluids. And outside the round of Society's events the new type of the coming decades was already beginning to emerge: the Bohemian. In 1900 Isadora Duncan, free-loving, free-dancing, came to London. By 1903 Augustus John was dressing his Dorelia in gypsy finery. By 1909 (the year Diaghilev and Bakst entranced Paris with barbaric costumes and dancing), avant-garde cliques of young things in Society and Cambridge were picking up the Bohemian style. It survived in country retreats and riotous Soho haunts of art students through the First World War, and emerged in time to take the fancy of the middle-class young of the '20s.

Bohemian dress is outrageously different, contemptuous of convention, escapist, theatrical: properties which make it attractive to rebellious students and which partly accounts for its triumphant revival by the pot-smoking generations of the '60s and early '70s. Many a flower-power girl waving her peace banner looked like Dorelia John, in her long, full skirt of cotton print, her suntan and her shawl. There was even

39 True Bohemia: Dorelia in 1909 in camp in Norfolk in her usual dress. The head-scarf, tied behind her straggling hair, the loose printed jacket and flashy velvet skirt worn with sandals and painted toe-nails remained her usual clothes for the rest of her life. Her strange, sly face was accepted by those in John's circles as extremely beautiful, but it was John who made them think so. She was as unlikely a beauty in her period as Jane Morris, with whom she had much in common.

a hint of her in 1983, in the dress of the peace women of Greenham Common. But in 1903 it was rather less usual wear than in 1968 for a legal secretary of suburban origin, as Dorothea McNeill was before Augustus John was taken by the gypsy possibilities he saw in her face.

It was not in the least like Lily Elsie's. 'Mysteriously, secretively beautiful', according to Ottoline Morrell, was Dorelia's pointed face, with its prominent cheek-bones, its slant, almost sly dark eyes, golden-dark skin set off by long straight hair, and a slight, Mona Lisa smile. It could never have looked at home above pastel-coloured chiffon, but it was perfectly designed to match the romany dress Augustus John delighted in. Within a couple of years of John's first meeting with Dorelia, mistress and wife were in flowing peasant dress, with a growing band of children to clothe as picturesque accessories.

96

40   Ida Nettleship, Augustus John's first wife, art student and daughter of Mrs Nettleship, who made Ellen Terry's stage dresses to Alice Comyns Carr's designs and ran a successful aesthetic dressmaking business in Wigmore Street. As striking in her way as Dorelia, Ida was neglected for her husband's new passion. She too wore gypsy dresses which she made herself to Augustus's ideas of the romantic and the Bohemian: with her background, she was familiar with the idea of a special dress for art.

Peasant dress was loose and unrestricting, dress it was possible to work in. Full skirts hung in paintable folds, with nothing in the way of petticoats beneath to hamper movement. Bodices clung close to the body's form and were fastened characteristically with buttons from a V-neckline to a normally placed waistline. The sleeves were cut loose enough at the shoulder for the arms to move freely about in, and the outfit was often finished off with an apron – not the useless, lace-trimmed, satin apron of the Society lady, but an ample length of printed cotton. Dorelia might be seen in a feathered hat (though the plumage might come from the farmyard) but she was as often to be found with a shawl over her head, and it is unlikely that she owned a pair of gloves of any sort. The whole effect was an outrage to conventional values.

Peasant working dress was approved of by the rational dress societies of the 1890s, and several of John's contemporaries thought Dorelia's

dress Pre-Raphaelite in style. It was neither, though there were trace-
able influences of aesthetic dress in the course of its evolution.
Augustus John's wife, Ida, who died in 1907, was the daughter of Ellen
Terry's aesthetic dressmaker, Mrs Nettleship. Though she seems to
have dressed in fairly normal clothes in the first years of her life with
John (except a burnt orange dress of seventeenth-century Dutch
influence in which she was painted when hugely pregnant), she was at
least used to the idea of a special type of dress for art, and for artists'
women. And she knew how to sew, making her own clothes and,
probably, some of the clothes for John's models, for they hunted
together for materials with which to decorate Dorelia.

There was a further Pre-Raphaelite influence from John himself, who
admired Burne-Jones's work in his youth and unfavourably contrasted
the upright bustled fashionables on Tenby promenade with his dream
women, diaphanously clad and delicately supple. In his case the Burne-
Jones influence, which is discernible in some of the clothes sketched in
his early work, was mixed with the influence of the costumes of fisherfolk and peasants which he sketched on the continent, especially in
France.

It was in their resemblance to the dress of working women rather
than nymphs of the marshes that the costumes of Dorelia and Ida, once
they had adopted gypsy life, were most astonishing to the contemporary
eye. Dorelia played the part of the intriguer, sending provocative
glances from beneath her feathered hats while Ida, weighed down by
babies and shawls, looks more earthy and less bewitching, although
her broad-nosed, full-lipped face, with its patient, large, dark eyes, was
equally unusual. Both adopted the rag-bag style of dress, for it was not
only desirable but necessary to choose clothes in which it was possible
to move and work freely in the conditions of a camp site, with a steadily
growing litter of John children to care for. Nothing was restrictive.
Dorelia's straight Chinese jackets hang loose, without interfacing, her
coats are dressmaker, not tailor-made, or she wears circular cloaks. The
necklines are cut low, in contrast to the high-boned collars of normal
dress of the time, which left red arrows round the necks of their
wearers. There are, of course, no stays or corsets. As a result of the
clothes and their lives, the poses of John's women are remarkably
modern. They slouch defiantly, Dorelia especially arrogant: hand on
hip, squatting on the ground with back curled and shoulders hunched.
The on-duty stiffness of the Edwardian Woman of Position is utterly
absent.

41 Blue Bohemia: Noel Oliver and Virginia Woolf (second right) at Clifford's Bridge in Devon in about 1908, with Rupert Brooke (right) and Maitland Radford. Blue Bohemia's holiday style was derived from the John example: they wore gypsy scarves, bare feet and casual clothes, and allowed themselves to become sunburnt. There was a lot of contact between the two groups of intellectuals and artists but on the whole, Blue Bohemia dressed fairly conventionally in town.

42 The Bohemians of the Edwardian era would have been perfectly in place at this pop concert in Hyde Park in 1971. The Bohemian revival of the 1960s and 1970s was mixed with an aesthetic one: the girl's cloak looks as though it is made from a Liberty print, and her hair is in the Morris idiom.

99

More revolutionary than these attitudes is the skin colour. The Johns were all dark brown if there was any sun about to turn them so. It is hard for the modern eye, after over half a century of tans, to appreciate the contempt this demonstrated for the values of the bourgeoisie or indeed the aristocracy. Even women who did have to work on the land attempted to protect their skin from the sun's humiliating rays. Dorelia bared hers to the sun defiantly, pulling her hair flat beneath her typical bright head-scarf, knotted back peasant-style beneath her hair. In Martigue in 1910 John painted Dorelia as suntanned as a native, extraordinary as that was in the days when Imperial prejudices still flourished.

No hat, no shoes: civilisation was capable of no further sartorial degradation except nudity. At least Dorelia does not seem to have taken her rebellion to those limits allowed to the children, who rushed around like savages in the grounds of their father's hired houses. What clothes were worn might bear obvious patches, from necessity and perversity. There was no respectable shift to make ends and appearances meet. Rather, a deliberate appearance of poverty was cultivated. The proudly-worn patch was to re-appear in the 1960s, but even in 1909 the egalitarian aspects of gypsy dress were finding enthusiastic admirers amongst the new-thinking, talented young at Cambridge. Fabianism was avant-garde and taught at summer camps. Camping out of doors, wearing John-type clothes and adopting attitudes of body and mind which had socialist overtones, was new, disapproved of, and therefore popular amongst enlightened adolescents. Rupert Brooke was an admirer of John. He visited him when the family camped at Grantchester and bought his work. His girl friends may be seen – Virginia Woolf, then Stephens, among them – sprawled on the grass wearing head-scarves, suntans and full skirts, and clutching teacups in both hands, while the odd Edwardian figure, stiff in lacy hat and blouse in the background, reminds us that this was far from usual behaviour. Fabian dogma predicted, according to Granville Barker, that women of the future would 'have dresses of the same material and wear them for the same length of time', though this pleasant picture evidently held less charm for the women of Brooke's circle than did the extravagances of Dorelia's dress. Ka Cox, Brooke's mistress, was invited to model by John and was close to both the artistic and the intellectual new movements of John and Bloomsbury, sometimes known as 'Blue Bohemia'. A Cambridge-educated girl, with more of the heavy maternal lines of Ida than the quicksilver graces of Dorelia, she flaunted kerchief and brightly-coloured peasant attire as her habitual dress.

But most of the women of Bloomsbury (other than Slade art students) and of the Grantchester circle of Cambridge seem to have adopted gypsy dishevelment only for informal occasions out of doors. It was almost their equivalent of the Society lady's country tweeds, and each naturally adapted it to her own style. Ottoline Morrell, another John model though hardly of his usual type, was called by the genuine peasants of Garsington 'Queen of The Gypsies' because of her habit of cycling round summer lanes in kerchief and flowing skirts. Typically, she had translated the mode into something richer and stranger: her dress was of genuine Russian linen, and the head-scarf was of silk. With casual dress (Brooke himself wandered around dreamily in open-necked shirts, hatless, a type of the coming man) came more casual manners. The Brooke set mixed unchaperoned and freely, and some-times even failed to change for dinner: the middle class was under attack from within.

Not all the pointers to change were in the John gypsy camp, of course. There were plenty of others, particularly from the more gentle, nostalgic kind of pastoralism which had continued to develop from its aesthetic beginnings. Its symbol was not the brash, defiant head-scarf but the more coyly romantic sun-bonnet. John loved peasant coifs, too, and Dorelia was sketched in one in Normandy in 1908, though the bold glance of the subject is hardly suited to the frame. Sun-bonnets were, however, in vogue amongst the older girls who formed the next generation from the Souls, jokingly known as 'The Slips'.

Lady Cynthia Asquith remembers wearing coloured sun-bonnets in the country, despite opposition from critics of the set, who claimed they looked 'musical-comedyish'. They looked especially odd when combined with the new manners of the new woman – smoking, for example, though in fact women had smoked in private by then for over half a century. Constance Collier, now working for Herbert Tree's theatre in the heart of that atmosphere which Mrs Patrick Campbell found so unnatural in 1909 – 'a disturbing mixture of domesticity and art, of Society and Bohemia, of conventionality and vagary, it irritated me' – picked up the pastoral escapist mood in France, where she stayed with Coquelin, the famous French actor, at Equihan, near Boulogne, where John had sketched the fisherfolk in costumes and sun-bonnets. Rising early, paddling in the sea, sleeping in hammocks in the garden, she lived the rural existence to the full and, despite her sun-bonnet, returned to England 'very much "in looks", very brown, from long days by the sea'. The notion that a deep suntan was connected with good health and beauty rather than poverty was years ahead of its time.

A centre of this kind of pastoral escapism existed at Smallhythe, in Kent, with links to the theatrical world, especially to Tree's theatre, and to the Souls. More surprising were the links to that least bucolic of publications, American *Vogue*. There, in the early years of this century, lived Ellen Terry, with her theatrical dress-designer daughter of feminist tendencies, Edie, nearby – the focus of a group of women interested in art, each other and the theatre. As might be expected of Godwin's daughter, Edie had her own ideas on dress. She was, of course, knowledgeable on historical costume, though the outfits she designed for her mother display her skills in theatrical effect rather than historical accuracy – by then an out-dated ambition for the stage designer. By the 1900s it was well understood that a rough hair-net of dyed string could be more effective beneath the lights than one of pure silk, knotted to the exact design of the Tudors. It was not for the stage, however, but for herself and her group of friends that Edie popularised the garment which was to become a classic of the twentieth century, particularly handy as servants became more expensive and the lady of resource was forced to do more in the garden than clip the heads of roses and more in the house than dust the most fragile porcelain. It was the now ubiquitous smock.

Ellen Terry had worn many smocked dresses during the years of the 1870s and 1880s, and Smallhythe was close to the area where the aesthetic dressmakers had once sent clothes to have smocking carried out by countrywomen who were still adept at the craft. But it was Edie who made the change from genteel smocking detail to the adoption of the actual, Bohemian smock for adult women, although a version had long been popular for children. She, Ellen and visiting friends wore real cream-coloured smocks and made-up versions of them, the nineteenth-century countryman's equivalent of the overall, over the blouses and skirts all day in the garden, changing only at night, for dinner. Easy, comfortable, worn without corsets, they represented liberation from convention and devotion to the higher thoughts of art and the nascent women's movement. There were very few men at Smallhythe (Ellen Terry's young husband was an exception much disliked by Edie) and this female group's evolved dress was at once thoroughly functional and un-sexy, even, since it was a male garment, rather rebelliously so.

Postcards of the elderly and now rather plump Ellen Terry wearing smocks over lace blouses spread the message to her British admirers, but the most powerful spreader of the new garment's popularity was *Vogue*. Not until 1916 was *Vogue* published in a British edition, and for some years after that it retained an element of American-prepared pages. But before that date copies were shipped to England, and there was a strong link in the text and pictures between American and English Society. Photographs of American heiresses who had married into the British aristocracy were prominently featured, and there were reports on the gossip of London. The particular link which provided *Vogue* with news of the smock and its origins was one of its artists, the Pre-Raphaelite-looking Claire Avery, a friend of Edie's. She lived on Long Island, with photographer Alice Boughton, who wore the Edie uniform – smocks, long skirts and no corsets. Both were friendly with Edna Woolman Chase, the ambitious and competent *Vogue* journalist who took over the editorship and saw her first issue in February 1914.

In May 1914 *Vogue* recorded, with a sketch by Claire Avery, the new trend in Long Island wear for the gardens, and its origins amongst the honeysuckle and beams of Smallhythe. These garments, however, had lost their rustic appearance and gained in sophistication: they were in bright, Bohemian colours, not the original porridge of the workman's smock. According to the anonymous and sly writer, they were the discovery of unnamed artists, who 'brought the smock habit back to America to their garden loving friends, who live in them during the Long Island summer, and bring them into town in winter. In town they wear them over respectable gowns as one wears an apron, but in the country each and every one of them wears her smock over a short skirt or baggy khaki trousers.'

That trousers were in these early years considered artistic and avant-garde (and not just the province of women war-workers) is supported by the fact that during the war Slade students sometimes turned up in corduroy trousers at Bohemian gatherings. The combination of smock and trousers was also to re-appear, with the smock in mini version, in the 1960s. *Vogue* suggested vivid colour combinations for smock-wearers – a yellow skirt and a green-blue smock, for example – and functional flat sandals to finish the outfit. For the summer issue of 1 July 1915 a version appeared on the cover, confirming *Vogue*'s support for the Smallhythe smock but this time in brilliant scarlet, with a blue and white striped long skirt, a wide-brimmed straw hat and a garden hoe. The smock's arty associations helped add romance to the chores for which it was so eminently functional, and this combination made it an irresistible garment for the twentieth-century lady. Ironically, the one

43　Pastoral Bohemia. A pre-war postcard of Ellen Terry in old age, with Marion Terry, in the garden at Smallhythe, Kent. The smocks and smock-like tops, worn over long skirts, were the idea of Ellen Terry's daughter, Edie, who was much involved in stage dress design and women's theatre.

use to which Edie and her girl-friends did not put it – maternity – changed it from its masculine rôle in the fields to one which epitomised femininity.　That there was a natural movement from an interest in art history as a source of inspiration for dress to an ethnic inspiration seems fairly clear. Even Mrs Newbery, isolated in Glasgow, had turned by the early 1900s from dresses taken from Carpaccio and embroideries after the manner of Morris, to Russia. Her students at the Glasgow School of Art were taught Russian needle-weaving, and she made regular purchases at a shop in London stocking Russian peasant crafts, run by a Mme Pogosky.

Russia was all the rage. Isadora Duncan visited it in 1904, ahead of her time as usual. Isadora embodied another aspect of Bohemianism: uninhibited movement, being important in the history of fashion not so much for her dress as for the scantiness of it. The art of wild gypsy dancing seems to have been one of the few subjects John omitted from the education of Dorelia, who preferred to sit withdrawn and slightly smiling while others cavorted. But for Isadora, movement was life. Her

104

44 The American *Vogue* version, derived from Smallhythe by Claire Avery and translated into smart garden wear for the May 1914 issue. It was a splendidly practical garb and soon became popular.

garments, it is true, were based on the purest aesthetic lines, a simply-draped Greek tunic, but the tunic was brief, the feet bare and the morals decidedly gypsy. Part of the interest of Isadora's dancing was the amount of her sturdy body it displayed: thighs, arms, sometimes even more, for her tunic was only held at the shoulders and attached to her body with elastic around the hips and waist. The anticipation and excitement this must have aroused in the audiences was rewarded on at least one occasion on her American tour of 1922, when one shoulder slipped with even more Greek effect to reveal a single bare breast.

The new dance style, based on the postures of dancers on Greek vases, along with a pair of dark eyes and a dimpled chin, proved a compelling combination for Gordon Craig, who saw Isadora dance in Berlin and provided yet another aesthetic link in Isadora's history: Ellen Terry's grandchild was one of the infants of Isadora who tragically drowned in the Seine. In 1906 Isadora was already known to Bakst and Diaghilev, and a host of imitators were copying her limber example,

45 Not a beauty, but wild in her ways and in her dancing, Isadora Duncan inspired troupes of Health and Beauty Leagues. Her dancing, partly based on the positions shown in Greek friezes, was done in bare feet and Grecian robes which occasionally fell off, to even greater pagan effect.

which was to launch many thousands of housewives across the world into tunics and barefoot Health and Beauty Leagues. In London one well-known dancer, part of Isadora's chain of influence and deriving much of her style from the Duncan example, was Margaret Morris. She had been trained in the basics of Greek dancing by Isadora's brother, Raymond, in around 1909, and soon began to hold classes for children in the subject, supplemented by summer camps. The First World War did little to slow her pace, and dancing continued in a teetotal club in London which John sometimes visited.

Free dancing, sunshine, health and fresh air were all associated in Margaret Morris's mind, no doubt in the tradition of the Greeks. Summer camps, for everything from scouting to socialism, were fashionable before the Great War, but Margaret Morris's progressive plans for a working vacation where it would be possible to dance outside with her pupils and 'bathe and lie in the sun', specifically for the purpose of turning a healthy shade of dark, were baffled by the rain of Devon until the war ended and she was able, in 1923, to rent accommodation for the summer cheaply in the south of France, at Eden Roc, near the Hotel du Cap. It was cheap because the south of France then had only a winter season, but Margaret Morris, with the connivance of the owner of the Hotel du Cap, quickly proceeded to change the seasons about. The owner, Mr Sella, saw an opportunity to manipulate the media and make money by filling his rooms in summer, so he invited Margaret Morris's pretty pupils into his ground and called in the photographers. 'We covered ourselves with oil,' says Margaret Morris in her memoirs 'and sunbathed on the flat roof of the Eden Roc Pavilion, and the press were invited to photograph my pupils diving off the rocks and dancing in the woods.' The publicity from the photographs prepared the way for Mr Sella's next coup: an invitation to some very cannily selected guests to come and spend the summer free of charge, and be photographed doing so, in his hotel. A guest list which included Picasso and Scott Fitzgerald, the Comte de Beaumont and a Russian ballerina resulted in some odd conversations over cocktails in the crucial first season of 1925, with Margaret Morris's dancers hidden a little way away in bungalows and appearing lively now and then on the horizon. But the commercially marketable aspects of Bohemianism were, through such masterly manoeuvres exploiting sex and snobbery, and the demand for good photographs in magazines, finally brought to the masses.

Isadora's dance was not only popular because it was sexually appealing. Women followed it because it was reasonably imitable, and because some form of exercise began to be necessary as lighter clothes made figure faults less easy to disguise by scaffolding. Mixed bathing hastened the demise of the very curvaceous female figure as the admired type. In America at the turn of the century the very rich had mixed bathing going on in their private swimming pools. It revealed by harsh sunlight that the mature woman, bereft of most of her clothes, could not compete in allure with the young. The body beautiful was bound to become fashionable, and the slim, straight figure, for which Ellen Terry and Sarah Bernhardt had in their youth been mocked, became a desirable prize.

The natural corset produced by muscle-tone was inevitably going to replace the unnatural cages of steel in time, but conventional prejudice made them survive even for sportswomen, where they were dangerous as well as unnecessary, for an absurd length of time. Even in 1919, the famous doubles player Elizabeth Ryan has told Ted Tinling, bloodstained corsets laid out to dry after the match were a familiar sight in the ladies' locker rooms of English clubs. They were not worn by the more ambitious and successful players, of course, and it was the ambition and success of tennis players like Suzanne Lenglen which defeated the corset for wear in even the most suburban of clubs.

A French champion at fourteen, Suzanne was the image of triumphant youth, and it was not her beauty which made her example in dress successful but her genius for tennis. Even as a child she was not pretty, and the sunshine she was exposed to on the tennis courts rapidly exaggerated the lines on a face drawn by stress: she had a hawk nose and unfortunate teeth. Nevertheless she was imitated in dress and in play. An Isadora Duncan of the tennis court, Suzanne leapt and pirouetted across it with a grace which came from constant ballet training. Her figure was enviably lithe and light and there was a considerable sexual element in her performance. As she whirled against the sunshine, her legs and figure were revealed: the skirt lifted to give glimpses of her thighs, bare above her long white stockings (held by garters) and even her breasts were sometimes seen as she bent down for a low ball. She was, as she grew older, well aware of the value of her many charms, but she was also conscious of the improvement ballet exercises had given her game. Inevitably, after retirement from amateur play, she became associated with the health and beauty movement, even working with Margaret Morris on a series of exercises specially for tennis players.

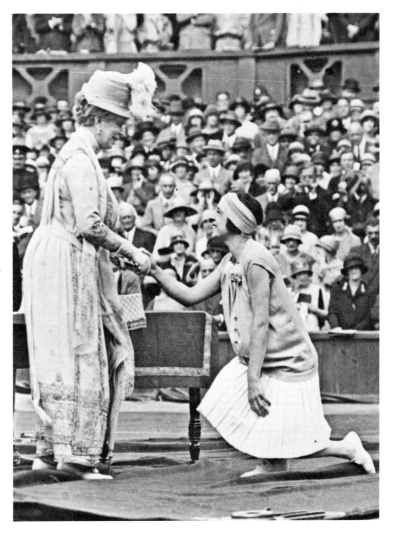

46 The improbable encounter of two ages: Queen Mary, firmly pre-war, and Suzanne Lenglen, dressed in bandeau, pleated skirt, coloured top (with her signature, a pinned flower) and flat white shoes. The photograph was taken at Wimbledon in 1926, but the dress is very similar to what Suzanne was wearing in 1919 when she startled the staid tennis world by appearing in see-through silks and showing her garters as she flew across the courts to victory.

Sex, success (she won Wimbledon in a famous victory in 1919) and spectacle were an impressive combination which made Suzanne the most copied tennis star in dress, but she was a populariser rather than an inventor. Other good women players had abandoned corsets, hats and restricting garments at least ten years before, though they lingered on for amateur players in suburban clubs. Suzanne's light dress went a stage further in shortness and transparency than that of other players of her prime, but it was partly intended to emphasise, by its youthfulness, her prodigy status.

As a child Suzanne played in full gathered skirts, calf-length, with the sailor top of the schoolgirl and a large bow in her hair. As a teenager, or nearly one (she was just turned twenty when she won Wimbledon), she wore a slimmer version with the sailor top simplified to an unadorned V-neck dress. The band in her hair (bandeaux were quite common for good tennis players, even men, before Suzanne made them famous) slipped over her forehead and grew in breadth and length to restrain her hair till the long scarf looked almost as wide as a head-scarf when wrapped round her brow. It was several years before day dress began to follow the natural logic which had produced Suzanne's sportswear.

But Suzanne's influence was not restricted to those who saw her in championship matches or read reports of her in the papers. She was part of Society's season, on friendly terms with the rich and royal, entertained by London fashionables during Wimbledon, and on every guest list for parties at the grand hotels during the Riviera's winter season, where her matches formed a kind of afternoon theatre. Not only did Suzanne have the social milieu in which to show off, she had attention stimulating her to do precisely that in dress and in behaviour – and she responded to it. The untidy little girl of early photographs developed into a temperamental star, draped in fur coats, wearing different bright cardigans and scarves for successive matches, bearing flowers from admirers pinned to her breast, and in silk tennis dresses ordered from couturiers. This glamour, which was her contribution to the sport, was probably as influential in making tennis a vital part of the social scene as were the clothes she wore for it. An ability to play tennis became as important to the middle class girl as piano-playing had been to previous generations.

But dress which did not hamper was being popularised indoors as well as out, before George V's Coronation. The Bohemian tango, originally a Spanish gypsy dance, had found its way to South America and back to North America and Europe, bringing a new wildness to the drawing rooms of Society. Its star was the boyish Mrs Vernon Castle, 'pioneer tangoist of America', as *Vogue* called her, the 'new woman' embodied, with a strong face and a free, swift walk, with her head held high, which was much copied. It was probably the necessity of a simple hair-style for vigorous exhibition dancing which made Mrs Castle bob her hair into a short, curly style much like Ellen Terry's of the 1870s and 1880s. This time other women discovered that its practicalities suited their own lives and bobbed hair, though daring, was much copied and tango teas were the rage.

To dance the fashionable tango it was essential to be fit, and desirable, though not essential, to be youthful. Chaperones took to the floor, and the term 'dancing mother' became a by-word. The old inflexibility on the type of dress which was suitable for a certain marital status and for different age groups began to bend. To be dressed simply was to be

110

47   Ellen Terry's hair-style appears once more, this time on Mrs Vernon Castle before the First World War. It was almost as popular as the gypsy tango, which she danced with boyish grace. Postcards like this enabled any girl to copy the style.

dressed in a younger and therefore more desirable style – like Mrs Castle, whose dresses, though feminine and flowing, were quite cleanly cut. Her combination of the naturally girlish and the fetchingly boyish, summed up in her un-dyed brown curls, was a powerful one. It is the type of the John Buchan heroine, slim, supple, strong and brave-eyed, but always quite clearly dependent on the hero – in Irene's case her husband and dance partner, who died in an air crash in 1918. It was not too radical an advance in image and so was acceptable to many women.

But it was Irene Castle's unfettered movement, not her naturalness, which was her only Bohemian quality. Bohemian women are, properly, garish, and in this respect can be most quickly distinguished from their aesthetic counterparts. Dorelia's fire-bright colours suited her dark complexion and gypsy style and they looked well out of doors where they were naturally placed, particularly in bright sunshine. Bohemians, unlike the aesthetes, do not dress for dim light or mysterious twilights. Flamboyant combinations of bright colours are their mark. Bright yellows, bright pinks, scarlet, violet-blue, emerald green, orange – all

111

these colours were worn in combinations by Dorelia, often set off by black velvet. Ethnic prints or bold stripes made it even harder to overlook her, though left to herself she preferred more subtle and quiet colours than those in which John liked best to see her. It was in bright colours that she was painted, and seen in art exhibitions, especially in the years before the war.

A brash dazzle was the effect the Bohemian aimed at, in dress and in jewellery. The meretricious, the tawdry or the exotic were approved of. Brass earrings were suddenly flaunted by art students. Dorelia wore green glass drops in her ears long before Coco Chanel made false jewellery famously acceptable. If the country gypsy liked to dazzle, the theatrical gypsy made it her profession. Indoors, for tango teas and for the ballroom, women followed the theatrical lead of Bakst and Picasso's harlequins. On the eve of the war, *Vogue* complained of the manner in which the tawdry was preferred to the true: 'Gorgeous gowns we have galore, but it is the colour and tinsel of the bazaar, not the stately richness of the salon.'

The appeal of the bazaar, or at any rate the backstage, is particularly strong for the romantic adolescent, and it is not surprising that by around 1910 the daughters of the Souls, or at any rate of Violet Rutland and Maud Tree, were embracing the new trends towards the bright and barbaric with passion. They had been brought up to scamper freely around His Majesty's theatre, encouraged to dress up in curious clothes and paraded in front of other children in the Van Dyck-ish artistic dresses which Mrs Haweis had recommended a quarter of a century earlier. As accessories to their mothers, they had learnt to expect to be different and to discount the opinions of 'other people'. It was only a step to enjoying outraging them.

It was natural enough that the new generation of Society aesthetes should most quickly pick up and transmit the new tendencies. What was interesting and different was that it was young girls who behaved in so shocking a fashion, debutantes, in fact, with a taste for low life and a habit of appearing in newspaper columns. Before the media ever invented the term 'Bright Young Things', Iris and Viola Tree and Diana Manners were inventing the kind of life-style that was meant by it.

Each had a very distinct image, which she cultivated with hallmark affectations. Least pretty was Viola – plump, large, rather clumsy, but allowed exceptional liberty for a gently-reared girl of her age because of her determination to make a career on stage, first as an actress then later, when that failed, as a singer. In 1910 she travelled alone, 'enveloped in a black cloak', to study singing in Milan, where she horrified the Italians by lying in the sun. Her freedom and her make-up box were envied by her little sister Iris, who spent long hours peering in the mirror, attempting to find a style which would win her attention: not an easy task in the shade of older, more beautiful and apparently more talented girls like Diana and Marjorie Manners. Iris succeeded by a series of dramatic gestures. When she bobbed her hair, which was straight and reddish-gold and hung in a mediaeval page-boy way which made it quite distinct from Irene Castle's curls, she left the sheared locks in her train compartment. Her pale face and weary eyelids were exaggerated by the use of make-up, which she kept out of Lady Tree's reach. Bright-coloured clothes were loved by both the Tree girls, who had a particular weakness for stockings. Viola went for bright green and red, Iris for different-coloured stockings on each leg in a parti-coloured look which was in keeping with her general attempt to emphasise her resemblance to a mediaeval jester or a harlequin. The group preferred the dressing-up box to the shop display as a source for clothes.

Violet Rutland had, of course, long preferred a self-invented style, and her daughter, Lady Diana Manners (later Lady Diana Cooper), followed her example. *Vogue* reports her (she was known in America almost as soon as she came out, in 1910) as having worn odd and artistic types of dress till about 1914, when she began to dress in more conventionally fashionable styles. But she never abandoned her preference for theatrical dress or, apparently, her scorn for 'good taste'. The *Vogue* type of seasonally changing fashion bored one whose natural style of dressing was flamboyant, inventive and untidy. Though she liked clothes and had a talent for dressmaking (she designed Viola Tree's wedding dress), she was baffled and wearied by constant descriptions of her as a leader of fashion and an arbiter of style. 'I know nothing about style,' she claimed. 'It's a joker word to me and I have none.'

But despite her disclaimers, Diana wore attention-seeking garments in public as did all the girls in the 'Corrupt Coterie', as the group was known. Impromptu, inimitable and unchanging, their style relied for much of its effect on audacity. In 1912, for instance, Diana marked her first visit to Venice by appearing in an Italian officer's white cloth cloak and a hat plumed with cock's feathers. In 1949 Cecil Beaton saw her don with undimmed enthusiasm a scarlet tricorne and red cape for a hunt ball at Chantilly. In 1979 the tireless beauty produced another variant of 'Diana the Huntress' for a fancy dress party held in her honour. It was

113

put together from a draped jersey Grecian gown, a long piece of tinsel ribbon to hold the stage-prop quiver of arrows, a gold hair-net and a wreath of green leaves over, which looked as though it had been twisted together that afternoon in the garden.

The carelessness of confidence is an irritatingly impressive characteristic. Society magazines and the popular press followed the movements of Diana Manners and her friends closely. A gift to the media, Diana was not only fashionably Bohemian in dress and behaviour, but a Duke's daughter and outstandingly beautiful. So lovely was she that Raymond Asquith wrote that 'it has given me the worst twinge I have had in the war to think of the children not turning round to look at you any more'.

But despite her apparent spontaneity, it was a beauty Diana worked to improve. For she longed as a child to be loved, and she had a need to collect compliments, common characteristics among beauties but rarely admitted to. White-faced, with wide, pale blue eyes and fair hair, she bleached her curls and back-combed them to make them more golden and thicker. The result was a radiant pallor. Contemporary descriptions repeatedly say that Diana 'glimmered', 'shone' or 'illuminated' rooms by her presence. She slimmed and exercised in the hope of growing thinner, and she developed a child-like trick of expression which she exaggerated for the benefit of any camera. With wide-opened eyes and startled brows, she would slightly purse her mouth and turn full face to the lens. She seemed to be at every party.

Attention of the kind which Diana Manners, Nancy Cunard and, to a lesser extent, Iris Tree received is a difficult drug to dispense with. None of them did. With them all it sprang in large part from genuine oddness and liveliness of character. They continued to turn heads, and they continued to be gay and gypsy-free in the gloomiest days of the war, partly with the help of champagne and, in Diana's case at least, morphine, to help anaesthetise them against the relentlessly growing list of friends and relatives who had died. Iris was only seventeen when the war broke out. She became a student at the Slade (Diana had taken

48 Daughter of two Souls renowned for their looks, Lady Diana Manners inherited her father's fair face and her mother's instinct for creative dressing. A comparison between this photograph and that of her mother, Violet Granby (page 77) shows that a talent for pinning laces, jewels and bits of material together into something which looks delectable may be handed down. The startled stare, the lifted chin and the slightly pouting mouth directed to the camera are part of a reaction so habitual it is now almost Pavlovian.

classes there in 1911, when the Dorelia mode was at its height) and, with her close friend Nancy Cunard, hired a secret studio in Fitzroy Street. They decorated it, like Diana's room at Belvoir Castle, in the colours of damnation, red and black. Slumped in pleasant squalor (Diana found it too frowsy for her taste), they planned new dresses and outings into low life. They met with John in cafés, drank beer in pubs, showed off their attitudes and clothes at Lady Ottoline's, slipped off to the Cavendish Hotel, drank absinthe and smoked. It all counted as disgraceful behaviour at a time when Diana's mother was forbidding her daughter, like any properly brought up young woman, to visit any hotel but the new and respectable Ritz. In Iris and Nancy's behaviour there was a good whiff of the delicious debauchery of the '90s.

While Iris's dress was, if not flowing, at least in bright Dorelia colours (Lady Cynthia Asquith records her at dinner in 1915 'very striking in black velvet with a large red leather bag'), Nancy Cunard kept her Bohemianism confined to her behaviour, her face and her jewellery. Stoat-thin, she had narrow eyes which she narrowed still more with kohl, an unhealthy pallor from night living, tight reddened lips and boyishly-cut golden hair which went well with her skimming walk, like Irene Castle's, hips thrown forward, head high. Leopard skin was fashionable in 1914 when Nancy was eighteen, but on Nancy's elongated figure it appeared unusually sinister, an effect only heightened by her narrowed, intensely-gazing eyes. She was not beautiful – her face was long, her mouth turned sadly down – but her poise, her elegance and her carefully taut gestures could make her seem so. The ivory bracelets, barbaric in themselves, which she adopted in the mid-1920s, served to draw attention to the length and thinness of her arms, and drew all ears as well as eyes as she gestured with her hands. Apart from them, her dress was remarkably simple, with the virtues of good cut, good material, refined rather than showy, with an American neatness and freshness which she may have inherited from her mother's side – though Maud Cunard is said never to have looked quite right in any of her expensive garments.

Though the fashions and fortunes of each female member of the Coterie continued to be followed by the press, the Coterie itself was extinct by the end of the war in which almost all its male members died. The women continued to surprise: Diana Cooper was the first Duke's daughter to take to the professional stage, in *The Miracle*, and to the screen, soon after the war. Iris, as ever ahead, bought her first pair of faded denims in 1924. Diana became so addicted to trousers that it was

49 Nancy Cunard, Bohemian and eccentric, took to wearing armfuls and throatfuls of African jewellery in the late 1920s. Her arms were a useful weapon in a quarrel. The little dress is perfectly normal, and as simple as *Vogue* could desire: the contrast between it and the rest of the outfit, not to say the mad, kohl-accentuated stare, is what makes Nancy's style so striking. Iris Storm, supposed to be modelled on her, claimed to have a pagan body and a Chislehurst mind, and if Nancy was similarly confused she expressed it with pagan accessories and a Chislehurst frock. Ironically, in face she closely resembled the person she loathed most in the world, her own mother Maud Cunard. To look in the mirror each morning and see your enemy evolve from your youthful face must be depressing enough to drive any woman to outrageous jewellery. It is interesting to note that Cecil Beaton did not bother to iron his back drops.

50 The green hat 'pour le sport' and a challenging stare, suggesting a sexual promiscuity to match it, worn by Tallullah Bankhead in the 1925 production of *The Green Hat* at the Adelphi. Said to be based on Nancy Cunard's stylish dressing and sexual freedom, the character of Iris Storm, wearer of the hat in question, brought to the public via the book and the play suggestions of a Bohemianism of behaviour in smart circles which was as stimulating as it was shocking.

117

51 In old age Dorelia John, like Jane Morris, did not desert her original style of dress. Shown here in 1950, Dorelia is still sunburnt, still fey-looking, still dressed in bright cotton with a flowing skirt and a natural waistline. She looks as convincing and distinguished a gypsy as she did in her youth.

feared, when her husband was appointed Ambassador to France after the Second World War, that she would wear them in the Embassy and shock the locals. But the effect of the constant publicity of the Coterie's doings before the war, the stream of photographs, of portraits, of newspaper reports and Society magazine tittle-tattle, now much more sophisticated and well informed than before, was to bring Bohemianism to meet the duller sections of Society and the middle classes in the 1920s. Debutantes with the staidest family connections began to wear obvious make-up, pursue treasure hunts around London in fast cars and wear glass bracelets and huge fake pearls.

By 1924 even *Punch* had noticed that Dorelia was in fashion. John exhibitions were praised by all, and elements of the dress she wore began to creep into the leisure dress of the more advanced middle classes. As, in the mid-1920s, suntans became desirable, the head-scarf was seen as a sensible way to protect a perm while leaving the face to

118

52 Meanwhile the button-front cotton dresses, not dissimilar to those which Dorelia was wearing half a century before, are adopted by royalty. Casual dress can go no further. Princess Margaret in British Honduras in 1958 wears a head-scarf (only this one is silk) and a bright, informal dress; even her behaviour at home had a touch of the Bohemian about it.

frazzle. It was totally unacceptable on Bond Street, but happily worn on a beach or a yacht. Casual dress gradually spread, though there was opposition. Gertrude Lawrence, healthily suntanned, created a stir when in the mid-1920s and a Broadway success, she was caught going aboard the *Mauretania* with bare legs. The papers excitedly reported it as a fashion Miss Lawrence was attempting to start, but Miss Carmel Snow, fashion editor of *Vogue*, was quoted as saying coldly, 'The idea is disgusting. It will never be done by nice people.'

The Second World War made head-scarves and bare legs a matter of necessity, and the head-scarf finally came full circle and reached a pitch of bourgeois respectability when in the 1950s it was inalienably associated with royalty. Princess Margaret and Queen Elizabeth could be seen in cotton dresses buttoned up the front which were very like shortened versions of Dorelia's, worn with or without head-scarves, for holiday and recreational wear. Bohemia could not penetrate much further.

6
Beautiful and Bizarre

Heads turned in the street in 1920 to follow the tall figures of Ottoline Morrell or Edith Sitwell: the first perhaps in heavy, pale yellow silks, with a large picture hat and a swoop of veiling; the second in a tapestry dress squarely cut with bell sleeves and a high waistline, topped with a green jacket and some religiously-shaped felt hat. But those who gaped could not be said to have been looking for fashion tips to follow. Paradoxically, the more original and creative a woman's dress is, the less likely is it to be copied – it is too radically individual. Sitwell and Morrell amazed and amused their contemporaries, but introduced no fashions in bizarre attire unless Edith Sitwell's claim that she popularised gold and silver nail varnish (which her dead white hands enabled her to wear with panache, but few can successfully imitate) is true.

They may have a stronger effect on future fashions, for their images continue to haunt the imagination more powerfully than the pictures of contemporary ordinary dress. Cecil Beaton's photographs of Edith and Baron de Meyer's of Ottoline could easily inspire a designer or a socialite to imitation in the next few decades, as Rossetti's studies of Jane Morris produced a flood of fashion copies in the early 1970s.

In every period there are women who dress eccentrically. In the 1910s and 1920s there seems to have been more bizarre dressing than usual, which suggests that eccentricity itself was a reflection of the period. As Doris Langley Moore commented, those 'who wear clothes which depend for their charm on a picturesque or dramatic line rather than upon the season's novelty' usually only imagine that they are being new: 'the taste of one's time has an insidious and inescapable influence.' A taste for oddness and extravagant display was part of the mood of the times. There is plenty of evidence to suggest that the more quietly-attired relished others' peculiarities. Diana Cooper recalls that the Marchesa Casati, living up to her reputation and 'drifting down the Grand Canal under a parasol of peacocks feathers', was a sight of Venice, like the lions. Those who knew Ottoline Morrell appear to have done little other than talk about her 'strangeness', just as present New York Society delights in the clownish make-up and Christmas tree jewellery that the ex-editor of *Vogue*, Diana Vreeland, has affected for years.

There are many reasons why women adopt a style of dress which startles. For Edith and Ottoline much of the explanation lies in their profile and their height. Both of them wore quite ordinary clothes at various periods in their lives, and photographs show that they look almost more peculiar in those than in the exaggerated styles they invented for themselves. Women who are merely plain, like Gertrude Lawrence, with her duck-beak nose and small eyes, can create an effect of prettiness by the use of cosmetics, accessories and the tricks and mannerisms of the much-pursued. Ottoline and Edith (like Diana Vreeland) could never hope to be called pretty. Handsome or beautiful they might have achieved, but their faces were too strong for sweetness. Ottoline had a large, long aristocratic nose, a jutting jaw, full lips and pronounced cheek-bones; she looked more like a Roman youth than an Edwardian lady. Edith's face was long, translucently pale, bony and high-browed, dominated by a sharp nose and high, arched brows. She looked, and she was proud of the fact, like a Plantagenet effigy.

As a result, they could hardly escape notice. Diana Cooper, in high-wayman's cloak and tricorne, would look charming, her glorious face making every dress seem correct for her and for her time. In the same clothes Edith or Ottoline would look extraordinary, like something from a different age or even a different world; Lady Cynthia Asquith records bumping into Ottoline in 1917 'looking like a nightmare'. Those with odd looks become used to being stared at. To court more stares by strange dressing may be an act of defiance, not just defence. Edith and Ottoline both felt isolated by their appearances, and in both their cases their looks made their childhoods more miserable. Ottoline suffered further because her mother made her dress differently from other little girls, whom in any case she rarely met, probably in some version of aesthetic attire.

A lonely child finds it difficult to pick up the unwritten rules and tricks of dress which the child of a large family or many companions finds come without conscious thought. Princess Alexandra knew instinctively what would be correct for any occasion, what might provoke laughter, what the judgement of others would be and, to an inch, where her jabot's bow should spread. Edith and Ottoline, with no girl-friends or sisters to instruct them, grew up without ever having developed an understanding of group dressing. It was a deficiency which made Ottoline unhappy. Somehow, she realised, whatever she did looked odd, there was no help for it. Even a stay at a Souls' house, Mells, nest of artistic Horners, only demonstrated how far she was from that which was acceptable even to aesthetes. 'I packed my best dresses,' she writes mournfully, 'which somehow, when shaken out and worn, seemed absurdly fantastic and unfitting for the company and the surroundings. Those that at home I was so proud of and thought so lovely would suddenly be transformed into tawdry "picturesque" rags, making me feel foolish and self-conscious in wearing them.'

Both lonely and intelligent girls were brought up in great houses, Ottoline in Welbeck, Edith in Renishaw, and it was natural that both should retreat into fantasies about the past, and about the portraits which surrounded them and the type of rich brocades and romantic headgear which they saw in those paintings. They both had faces which might have been fashionable in past ages, and the past is a safe place to be: it cannot reject. Ottoline, disappointed by the lack of accuracy and imagination shown in a historical fancy dress ball she attended, reflected that it was possible that she was a 'rare survival', someone at sympathy with 'the time of hoops and loops and billowing skirts'. Dressing up was a game neither ever abandoned, though they chose opposing types. Edith identified with the ambitious Elizabeth I, Ottoline with the more dreamy and tragic Mary, Queen of Scots.

Golden dresses, huge gems to display the fragility of her long white fingers, materials chosen for theatrical effect, stiff robes: these were all features of dress that Edith had in common with her heroine. Her face was strikingly like Elizabeth's, whose entry into London on the Saturday before her Coronation she describes in *The Queen and the Hive*: 'a straight and narrow figure in a cloth-of-gold dress, under a cloth-of-gold mantle with an ermine cape. From a gold circlet, limp strands of red-gold hair fell down, framing the delicacy and strangeness of an oval, pale face, a face with faint brows spanned like Norman arches and heavy-lidded golden eyes, smiling at them.' The face, hair and eyebrows were all in the mirror for reference. And like the young Princess, Edith had early decided upon a need for attention: her brother, Sacheverell, thinks that she had made up her mind by about the age of fifteen to be a public figure.

Ottoline had no such ideas. She simply indulged her own ideas of beauty, wore her romantic pearls which reminded her of Mary, Queen of Scots and Marie Antoinette, loved finery and rich effects, and was

53 & 54   Art imitating Art. Coward's skit
on the Sitwells was well received by
all except the subjects of the satire. His
version of Edith's dress, a sack-like tunic
with clusters of improbable fruit hanging
from her ears, a head-scarf and several
strings of tribal beads, had, like all
caricatures, a degree of truth hidden in it.
In the Baron photograph, taken in
1956, Edith wears almost as unlikely an
outfit with a stiff brocade cloak, a primitive
collar and a knotted head-scarf beyond
even Coward's imagination. But by this
time Edith Sitwell was no longer a crazy
and possibly dangerously progressive
curiosity, but one of the nation's
cherished eccentrics.

surprised by other people's wonder at her fantasies of the past. Aristocratic backgrounds or immense wealth are great provokers of eccentricity, and Ottoline and Edith had the blood, if not the money, to help them realise their dreams of dress. Money and a dream of past grandeur inspired Mrs Rita de Acosta Lydig, descended from Spanish nobility and divorced from a millionaire, to live out her re-creation of the golden age in New York before and during the First World War in something of a similar, but much grander, style, to that of Edith and Ottoline. She too despised fashion and favoured old brocades, wearing high lace collars with a look of a princely boy, or sometimes of Elizabeth I. Pale (she used lavender powder to give her an eerier pallor still), with a small poised head and a humorous mouth, she was also painted and sculpted for posterity's amazement, though she was much more acceptably beautiful than either of her British counterparts.

Edith and Ottoline had to overcome more obstacles to win the title of beauty, but they were both called by the cognoscenti beautiful in their own strange and mysterious way. In Edith's case it was achieved partly by directing attention to a face others more cowardly might have attempted to soften. For the best of the bizarre dressers, compromise is anathema. Edith's 'green-gold' hair, one of her instantly recognisable beauties, was hidden away much of the time in turbans and exotic hats, so that on first meeting her, Virginia Woolf doubted whether she had any. Ottoline used bold hats of immense size to draw eyes to her decisive profile: an advertisement once seen on the village notice board at Garsington, where Ottoline had a permanent plea pinned up for lost head-scarves, silk gloves and the like which she had scattered around Oxfordshire, was for a busby of white bearskin, three feet high, that she had somehow mislaid.

The peril of such an approach is that it treads a narrow line between art and caricature: it is not surprising that portraits of the two are frequently less than flattering or even truthful. It takes a bold eye to see one's own highlighted oddness further exaggerated by the artist. Augustus John's painting of Ottoline, grimacing like a mad horse, was so strong that it impressed even the artist when Ottoline had the courage to hang it in her dining room. The *Sketch*, reviewing the exhibited work on 12 May 1920, found it so breathtakingly impolite that its amazement was expressed chiefly in dots: 'Surely Lady Ottoline Morrell can hardly . . . I mean . . . well, really . . . people couldn't bear . . . it *can't* be true.'

A mixture of humour and pride is the bizarre's best defence.

55 Margot Asquith, a woman who made no concessions, least of all to her own profile. Frantically keen on high fashion, she dressed to the minute with ludicrous results, and her evident self-satisfaction makes the result the more peculiar. Had Margot adopted more of an individual style she might have seemed, paradoxically, less bizarre.

Sacheverell Sitwell was asked by Lady Ottoline during one dinner what he thought of the portrait under which she was presiding. To his polite reply to the effect that it seemed a reasonable likeness came the astonishing remark, 'You don't think it too chocolate box, do you?' Elizabeth Salter, Edith's companion in her last years, remembers that Edith disliked being called 'plain', much preferring to be 'ugly', and claimed that her stylishness was equally extreme: 'If one is a greyhound, why try to look like a pekinese?'

As extreme was Margot Asquith who, though she wore strictly fashionable and up-to-date attire, nevertheless managed to look most peculiar on all occasions. The cause was partly her large-nosed and tooth-dominated face, but chiefly that she refused to acknowledge in her dress or behaviour that she was not a beauty in her time. On the few occasions when there are hints that she did recognise this truth the effect is also odd, and she must be one of the few authors of memoirs to have used a back view of herself as a frontispiece (in *More Memories*).

Rouged to the hilt – Lady Cynthia Asquith, her step-daughter-in-law, described her in July 1917 as 'a painted skeleton' – she kept her slim figure, if not her face, by will-power. She subdued all around her, including the gossip writers of the *Sketch*, who described her meekly and truthfully in June 1920 as 'always a striking figure at all social functions'. Unusual sartorial effects, like the wearing of ankle socks with afternoon frocks, were her particular speciality, and she was always anxious to keep up a high standard of dress for the sake of the living or the dead,. When asked by Lady Cynthia whether she would be wearing the ostrich-feather hat for Kitchener's Memorial Service she replied with astonishment, 'How can you ask me? Dear Kitchener saw me in that hat twice!' Her face is not dissimilar to Lady Ottoline's, but Ottoline's solution to it, just as uncompromising, was much more romantic and attractive. Nevertheless, they both shared in full measure with Edith Sitwell the necessary virtue of a stylist: confidence.

Edith knew from an early age that she wanted to look different from other people, and not at all like the pink and pouting beauties her mother and father admired. In typical adolescent style she went first for black: black velvet and jet rings to show off the white fingers which were and remained exceedingly beautiful – so much so that she once used a picture of them as a Christmas card. But it was her elder brother, Osbert, aesthete and devotee of the Ballet Russe, who suggested that she should wear brocades cut in plain and simple style, and it was Osbert who gave her the hangings for her unfashionably situated flat, hangings of green and silver for her companion's sitting room and of red and gold for her own, to form a suitably splendid background to Edith's new clothes. It was a theatrical background, in a theatrical period (she moved into Bayswater in about 1913) for Edith's theatrical dress. That the prime motive was dress as a setting for the wearer rather than a thing of beauty in itself is suggested by the dresses which survive. Like her flat, they were more striking in immediate effect than in the quality of their details. Edith was short of money for much of her life, but it is not simply poverty which sends a woman to a furnishing shop to buy her brocades when antique fabrics could be found with an effort. Unlike Ottoline, who adored fine sewing and sumptuous fabrics, Edith does not seem to have been at all concerned with the quality of material or standards of finish. Her dresses – wool or brocade for day and brocade or velvet for the evening – seem to have all been cut on much the same pattern: a square neck, bell sleeves, a highish waist (later dresses are sometimes cut without a waist seam) and a gathered skirt to ankle length. Those for evening might be longer, with a pleat at the back to form a psuedo train from the waist. Roughly finished inside, fastened with zips and hooks and eyes, they are not the dresses of a woman who loves costume for its own beauties.

Most of her dresses in the early years were made up out of materials from Sheffield by the local dressmaker near Renishaw, or in the village at Weston. Even when, richer from the success of her books on Elizabeth and later anthologies, she patronised a King's Road dressmaker, she was brief in her commissions, asking only for less braid than last time, or for a higher neck because her vest kept showing. Dresses were to be seen in, not to waste time on that could be better spent in more creative fields. She liked clothes with drama, swirling cloaks, dead black to emphasise her white face, blue and pale gold brocade which matched her hair, the bright yellows, blues and scarlets of the '20s, tricorne hats, turbans and strange, squat hats from department stores which her face transformed into objects of speculation and mystery. There was a brief phase in 1930 when her face and her hands plumpened out into fat and the bones were lost, but Edith simply tied her head in a scarf and looked like a sinister Pope.

Her jewellery had a barbaric flavour that was distinctly of Bakst and of the '20s, too. Virginia Woolf vulgarly supposed that Edith's habit of wearing enormous jewels sprang from a desire to compensate for the tawdriness of her flat, but though display of person was Edith's concern, display of wealth was far beneath her. The enormous size of her pieces – one ring was about as long as her little finger, and of two fingers' width – gave an intentionally stagy effect and some were actually of paste. Their archaic flavour complemented her curious dress. Her rings were sometimes worn, Renaissance-style, two to a finger, and one of her necklaces, of three pieces of beaten metal shaped like axe-heads, looked as though it had been found in some primitive tomb.

The influence of Russian theatrical splendour, first brought to her by Osbert, was given a second wind in 1930, when Edith met and fell in love with the beautiful Pavel Tchelitchew, who designed some of her clothes for her. (Her love was, as befits the romantic, entirely unrequited.) Tchelitchew had previously worked on stage costumes for *Le Coq d'Or* for the Russian State Opera in Berlin in 1923, and he saw in Edith not only a macabre face to draw but a figure whose mode of dress he entirely understood.

During the First World War she was in contact with some other poseurs of the period, including Iris Tree and Nancy Cunard (to whom

56 Edith Sitwell in ecstasy, prepared for an audience, being filmed at the Phonofilm Studio in 1927. The veiled hat was a favourite, worn for at least one portrait and some Beaton photographs. The brocade dress and large rings on her deliberately displayed and very beautiful hands are typical of her 'stage' style.

she seems to have been referring when she wrote of 'a vulgar little clothes moth') but she does not seem to have been impressed either by them or the women of Blue Bohemian Bloomsbury, whom she thought dull, with faces like fawn hats that had been sat on. She was one of those very shy women who has the complete conviction of her superiority in most matters, though she did admire Virginia Woolf, whose face, lit up by intelligence, she described as having a moonlit beauty.

As her period and her part demanded, Edith painted. Her hands received careful attention in the way of manicures and polish, and her fingernails were worn long and cut slightly pointed as befitted the shape of her pencil fingers. Her eyebrows were plucked into a line which made their startled height even more distinctive, her eyelids were glossed, in the early photographs, like those of Paula Gellibrand, and shadowed with colour to emphasise their deep sockets.

57   But even Edith Sitwell did wear normal dress at times and, as the photograph taken at a wedding in 1929 shows, looked almost as strange in it, like a bird of prey, as she did in her more inventive clothes: the profile dominates.

Theatrical dressing naturally requires a stage, and Edith was at her happiest when she was either on one or in the lens of Cecil Beaton, who found her his best subject. With his camera's attention trained on her she looks utterly relaxed, the mouth happy, the eyes wide, the hands dropping into their natural pose, fingers of one spread over the wrist of the other. Her stiff, home-made-looking dresses are perfect camera props, striking and bold in outline, just as effective as when, lit on stage, she gave poetry readings in New York in 1948 in gold, or attended the concert to celebrate her seventy-fifth birthday at the Royal Festival Hall in red velvet and gold. Hers was a regal appearance (as Lady Macbeth, for a reading in New York in 1950, she even wore a crown) and, to compensate for her unhappy adolescence, her face rewarded her in age: her magnificent array suited her better the older she became. By the 1950s her name and her appearance had won her all the attention her teenage self had wished for.

58   Lady Ottoline Morrell by Cecil Beaton, in an evening gown made to her own romantic fantasy. Its full skirt would have looked better with a petticoat or two beneath it to fill it out and soften the line of Lady Ottoline's bony knees, a point she was in the habit of forgetting. It is, nevertheless, a charming dress, well suited to a strong, strange, almost Spanish profile. Pearls were her favourite jewellery, worn with almost everything she had.

Ottoline Morrell also dressed for a part, but not for an audience. A loner, intensely romantic and passionate-natured, she lived in and for her own imagination, the heroine of some historical myth which absorbed her. Chestnut-haired, with great dreaming eyes and a trance-like walk which fascinated D. H. Lawrence, she was vaguely and sometimes painfully aware of the impression she created on viewers, but it was only an awkward incidental. She dressed strangely because she loved her own idea of what was beautiful, and because she was extraordinarily sensitive to her surroundings and her personal surroundings – her costume. A child in the 1880s – her mother, Lady Bolsover, had friends in the artistic set – she was partly influenced by

130

the aesthetic movement. She sometimes wore floating draperies which made her tall figure look still more elongated, and she liked the effect of draping her face with a veil of chiffon or lace, or of tying scarves to flutter behind her as she drifted along in the other world she preferred to her present. The half-tone harmonies of the aesthetes remained favourites of hers too. Whistlerian yellows and greys, grey-pinks, grey-browns, green-blues, were nicely blended in her costume and her rooms. She had an excellent eye for colour, though she liked to introduce sunny Italian oranges, peaches and corals into her surroundings, too. Unusually for an Englishwoman, yellow became her. Not only did she make it the characteristic colour of her dress, she liked to arrange her rooms so that they had a yellow light from lamps, or through transparent taffeta curtains which helped provide some sunshine in grey weather.

But her taste was also for the '90s, or at least for the grotesqueries of the period. Her full-skirted dresses, worn with swirling hats and of highly-decorated fabrics, belong to the eighteenth century of Beardsley's illustrations for *The Rape of the Lock*, highly artificial, distorted, voluptuous. Such full-skirted dresses, often of taffeta, showed off Ottoline's best feature – her tiny waist – and gave curves to her slim, straight body. Like Consuelo Vanderbilt, she lost all proportion when dressed in droopy '20s clothes: she was too tall for them. Fantasy obsessed her, and it was of a story-book nature. Her shepherdess dress would be bowed, plumed and bedecked in the style of Marie Antoinette, not of rustic simplicity. Though she admired Dorelia's dress, she found encampment life distastefuly drudge-like and attempted to add a little gaiety to it with the gift of a Leghorn hat. Dreaming, rather than toil, was her idea of escapism. Her very stance was escapist, as recorded by John and by photographs: she stood with chin held high and hands spread back like wings behind her, like the figurehead of a ship or an angel awaiting assumption.

There was no attribute of the romantic which Ottoline omitted from her life. Her untidiness, a string of unrequited loves, her sensuality and her nostalgia all proclaim that her mind was on higher things than reality. Dress materials were cherished for their associations, and the patina of age was hallowed in her house and in her dress to such a degree that Henry James objected to her lack of New World freshness and her detractors accused her of wearing dirty clothes. Ottoline was amazed by criticisms of this kind. For her, worn brocades and faded garments were redolent of dreams of a past which had a more sym-

59 Lady Ottoline in pseudo-Grecian mood in about 1912. She had at least one other dress of exactly this cut, with the Grecian button sleeves, high waist and floating pointed panels of a different colour in what looks like silk. This dress may well be Ottoline's home-made copy of a Fortuny. It shows to advantage her slim, supple figure, one of Ottoline's several beauties of person which her circle never seemed to notice. She has matched her dress with a thin fillet threaded through her hair. Her intensity, very evident here, was what chiefly made her laughable.

pathetic and subtle sense of beauty than the machine-ridden present.

Unlike Edith, she enjoyed fabrics for their sensuous qualities: their crisp rustle, their satin sheen, the delicate softness of old lace. Sewing was for her an absorbing pastime of a kind which she thought suitable for a woman who loved beauty, and her coloured silks went with her on her honeymoon. She enjoyed collecting and wearing fine garments of the past such as Turkish, Arab and Persian embroidered finery, which she kept in trunks and which were available for any of her visitors, at Garsington or in Bloomsbury, to amuse themselves by dressing up in at her entertainments. Dressing and interior décor, she felt, were both arts, however minor, that were insufficiently understood or valued. 'I heap up beautiful things, oriental cloths, old embroideries, Italian damasks, painted silks,' she wrote in her memoirs.' If it were permanent I might be allowed to do it as artists paint their pictures, but they say it is ephemeral and soon passes away . . . I murmur to myself, "Birds' feathers are beautiful as well as convenantes, flowers are beautiful." '

Ottoline was carying on a long tradition of interest in Turkish costume. Lady Hester Stanhope had amused herself in the early nineteenth century in the same aristocratic, fantastic vein. In Turkish smoking hat and with cigarette in hand, Ottoline looks more boyish and Beardsley still with a suggestion that (like Vita Sackville-West) more simple, masculine dress might have suited her strong face better than feminine frills.

Byron's granddaughter, Judith Lytton, wore Arab costumes as usual dress, and in similar clothes Ottoline might have been a more striking and less ludicrous figure than in some of her more feminine garb. But Ottoline was, despite her face and height, an extremely feminine woman. She had adored her mother extravagantly, and she had no wish to stride about the country pursuing boyish adventures. If flowing skirts produced submissive attitudes, as so elegantly argued by Virginia Woolf in *Orlando*, Ottoline would spread her skirts more widely and accept the truth of it. Not that she dressed for men: much of her male acquaintanceship was undoubtedly embarrassed by her company in public (though it ought to be said that Ottoline was entirely unembarrassed by whatever her companions wore, however déclassé). Ottoline dressed for beauty. For its sake she was delighted to spend time looking in the looking-glass, staying and lacing, washing and powdering, changing like Orlando 'from silk to lace and lace to paduasoy'.

Inevitably, she dressed with most enthusiasm when in towns and houses she felt were sympathetic, though she might be seen innocently defiling the most sanctified of philistine territory by her ignorance of the unwritten rule, as when she was spotted riding in Rotten Row with a wreath of red roses round her top hat. In Oxford, or better still Venice (she regarded Italy as her spiritual home), she might let her fancy romp. Both were at that date grey cities, providing backdrops in various shades of her favourite wall colouring, high in 'atmosphere' and tolerant of dreamers. Ottoline, like Violet Granby, was not the kind of woman who preferred the hand of nature to be unrestrained by man's. Wild moors did not fill her with unutterable thoughts, as decaying buildings did. In Venice she might dress with negligence, with panels or long

133

scarves floating behind her. In Oxford, walking down the High, she might affect an eighteenth-century dress. In Garsington she might wear whatever she wished and feel that it blended perfectly with the surroundings she had created, with their Venetian pale green-greys and red lacquers touched with gold, and the scent of incense in the air. It particularly pleased her when two Society women, Baroness d'Erlanger and Mrs Lambert, came to call and gave her the unusual sensation of seeing someone else looking quite out of key: 'they looked so decorated and artificial, like two paroquettes in our rural black and white Breughel scene.'

Both Edith and Ottoline were expressing themselves, however odd those selves were, in their costumes. Neither of them was subdued by the disapproval or laughter of the majority. Perhaps because they did not understand the rules and operation of a group, they seem to have been especially disliked by those who were in 'sets'. Ottoline was disapproved of by the Coterie, despite their supposed admiration for eccentricity of behaviour and appearance, and was mocked by much of Bloomsbury, who also found Edith's strangeness made them uncertain of their own taste. There were always those independent judges, more confident and more discerning, who saw not only the bizarre beauties of these two faces but the humour and innocence which brought them alive.

Partly through the caricature of the former groups, as well as the records in writing, on canvas and on film of the latter, the images on which the two women spent so much effort have been preserved. The dichotomy between the two is partly responsible for the legendary quality those images have already assumed. Probably that is what both of them would have liked, for they shared an odd but marked sense of humour.

7
The New Lady

By the mid-1920s the rebellion against respectability was beginning to lose its impetus. Although the middle classes were still enjoying Bohemianism, erstwhile genuine Bohemians, like Lady Diana Cooper, were dressing more like 'other people'. Duff Cooper stood for Parliament in 1924 and sartorial eccentricity is not a desirable quality in an MP's wife, so Lady Diana was to be seen in the soft pretty dresses given to her free by the designer, Ospovat. Back in America in 1925 for her *Miracle* tour with Iris Tree, she wrote to her husband from Boston on 25 October, 'It's midnight, and over our delicate supper Iris and I discuss the change of conditions and desires in ten years. What would we not have given for a privacy like this, unhaunted by mothers and maidenheads? Here we have time, space, a cellar and fullest freedom, and we discuss it before retiring early.'

To be lady-like in appearance was once more to be fashionable, but it was a stylised, sophisticated version of the look. It was not quite as natural and confident as the kind of lady-like style Princess Alexandra had exemplified, for there was an element of defensive extremism in it. So many families were losing lands and houses, Society was so clearly insecure, that it was necessary to fall back on unwritten rules for protection. Ostentation in dress was associated with the vulgar and the nouveau riche, simplicity was associated with good birth and breeding. As early as 1920, therefore, the snobbery of simplicity was in the air. The *Sketch* ran a little social cartoon about Angela, a well-brought-up gel, forced to work for her richer inferiors, the fat and flowery Excess-Profitts, advising them on etiquette. 'She is explaining,' runs the caption, 'that if they want to impress the County they should not wear satin garments trimmed with diamanté – particularly in the morning.' Angela's grandmama, who came down to breakfast in velvet at country house parties, would have been quite surprised by her descendant's severity.

Lady Diana never quite managed to rid herself of a certain flourish and disarray in her dressing, even in this period. Those who exempli-

60 Utterly ladylike, Lady Diana Cooper appears for a polo match in 1924 in slim chiffons, shady hat and pearls – the perfect future MP's wife.

fied the lady-like style best dressed in a crisp, controlled, pitilessly plain manner. *Vogue* preached the virtues of the little black dress in 1925, and by 1926 it was a regular sermon: the way to chic was to strip off all bangles, fake flowers, drop-earrings and glitter, leaving the plain satin shift and a single-strand necklace which was all a lady needed in the evening.

It was not necessary to be a lady in breeding or behaviour to adopt the new style. The paradigms, in looks and success, were not as they seemed to the eye. Lady Ashley, for example, with soft blue gaze, white skin, fair hair and curved, submissive stance, dressed with admirable restraint and appeared to be the perfect English aristocratic girl. Formerly Sylvia Hawkes, she was in fact believed to be the daughter of an ostler, but neither this nor her husband's family's fury at the mésalliance stopped her from achieving her first tiara and then abandoning it for the hands in marriage of Douglas Fairbanks, Lord Stanley of Alderley, Clark Gable and Prince Djerjazde. Sylvia Hawkes looked more like the real thing than many an Hon. tramping round the shires: the stylised lady was, in fact, a little too perfect to be true.

136

To keep up the standards of perfection which absolute neatness and simplicity demanded, it was necessary to be near a town, preferably a capital, where hairdressers and beauty salons abounded. Town-sharp dressers do not feel happy near mud. Thelma Morgan Converse was decidedly an exile from her own territory when her future husband, Lord Furness, took her to his isolated shooting lodge and introduced her to a daughter whose walk, Thelma disapprovingly noted, 'gave me the impression she would be happier in a riding habit than in a ball gown'. Thelma herself, and her twin, Gloria Vanderbilt, walked with most assurance in London, Paris, New York or the south of France, in all of which places they were noted for their style: a highly groomed, cosmopolitan chic developed from a childhood spent in European capitals (their father was an American diplomat) and further polished by their dual debut in New York Society, aged sixteen and un-chaperoned. With dark, shining hair and creamy skins, they had a composure and elegance which entirely compensated for their rather long and irregularly-featured faces. 'Perhaps,' they ventured in their

61   Lady Furness in 1933, confident, beautifully dressed, in clothes which match, fit and hang properly. No awkward smiles from her, and no careless slips like Mrs Royston's, who is letting her stocking heel show. A similarity between her crisp style of dress and Mrs Simpson's later manner (see page 153) is evident. They had a lot in common, including American birth and the Prince of Wales.

joint memoirs, 'we had a talent for creating an illusion of beauty. . . . We had a style of our own.'

Of the two, Thelma had the most presence, but both were good examples of the Long Mirror Look – that kind of beautifully co-ordinated style which is the result of hard work and careful study of the looking-glass. Their hemlines were arrow-straight, shoes polished, clothes pressed; the whole effect was of hat and outfit and shoes in perfect proportion and effortlessly teamed. They had maids, of course, and wore designer clothes, preferring Vionet, Chanel and Lanvin in Paris and Sonia Rosenberg in New York, with hats from Reboux, but so did other women who looked drab beside them. Thelma and Gloria made more effort, wore their clothes with more assurance, chose more striking combinations of dark and light colours, and found lines which suited them, especially vertical ones, which made them seem taller. They wore their satiny hair parted in the middle and sleeked very close to their heads, so that the waves scalloped down the sides of their faces, which were powdered even whiter to contrast. In the evening they wore very plain, satin dresses which flowed about them. Their gestures were gracefully controlled. All this combined, in Thelma's case, with a slightly strained face and a dark, intent gaze could make her a little hard-edged in appearance; it may only have reflected her personality, for it was Thelma who had the coolness to keep her ciné-camera running, for example, during an incident when out lion-hunting in Nairobi and so got a 'wonderful, though rather harrowing, shot of a native boy being clawed by one of the lions'.

The particular lion Thelma had her attention on in the early years of the '30s was the Prince of Wales who, a dandy himself, admired female dandies. The fashionable dresser of the period was as usual very much the type the Prince preferred, and Thelma was dark, confident and clothed in much the same crisp style as his previous mistress, Mrs Dudley Ward. It is a mode well suited to the slight and small, which was the first requirement for all the little Prince of Wales's loves. They had met in the country, at Leicester Fair, where he first asked her for dinner without Lord Furness, but that was the only rural note in their relationship.

From then on it was at night-clubs, dances, cocktail parties and charity events that gossip writers and fashion editors noted the important details of Lady Furness's clothes for their readers. Of all social occasions, the cocktail party, essential feature of the smart '30s, serves the stylised dresser's purpose best. There is plenty of light, so that clothes and jewellery may be seen, and opportunity to compare and stare. Least enjoyed are out-of-doors entertainments, where the elements make it more difficult to keep up standards and the light source is uncontrolled. The best dressers of the '30s were probably at their happiest in the entirely artificial surroundings of transatlantic liners, with beauty salons, hairdressers and an endless and quite predictable social round to dress up to. It was on a liner in 1934 that Lady Furness tangled with the Aly Khan and, as a result, lost the Prince of Wales.

Not a stylised version of a lady, but the genuine article, was Princess Marina, who married the Duke of Kent in 1934 in a white and silver princess-line dress with a draped neckline and trumpet sleeves which was a triumph of understatement, especially for a royal bride. She could compete in poise and flair for dress with any of the town brass, having spent some of her life in Paris, but she could also look perfectly at ease in country tweeds and even appear charmingly untidy. Cecil Beaton saw a film of the King entertaining at Balmoral and noted how, while Mrs Simpson looked too smart, Marina 'looked romantic with her hair untidily blowing and tied with a baby-bow of ribbon'. Her manner of dressing, like her great-aunt's, Queen Alexandra's, was the entirely natural result of a love of clothes and an instinctive understanding of what was appropriate. Like Alexandra too, she could look very beautiful in simple evening dress, but she tended to load herself with family jewellery appropriate to her husband's status and her own, including a huge and hideous diamond bow.

With a long, lop-sided face and quizzical eyes, Marina was hardly beautiful. When it stiffened before the cameras she could look much older than her years, but for people she had a mischievous and spontaneous smile which illuminated it. She looked at her best in motion, eager and amused. Her own kind of loveliness was not at all hard-edged or brittle, and she softened the fashions of the '30s into a more nostalgic image. Where Margaret Whigham in an afternoon hat looked unambiguously contemporary, Marina had an echo of Anna Karenina. Her lipstick was less dark than the mode, her eyebrows their natural shape, her stance slightly retiring rather than defiant, her waved hair its natural gentle brown. The tilted smile was generally matched by one of the tilted hats she was famous for (the 'Marina hat' in the year of her engagement was a pillbox with a peaked top, but a succession of fetching headgear followed, all eagerly chronicled by news photographers on every royal visit), the long throat encircled by pearls. It

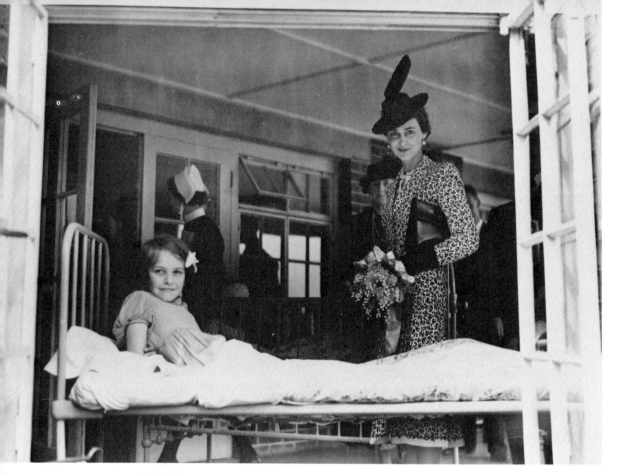

62 & 63   Tilted hats, earrings, pearls at the throat: a familiar look. Princess Marina, Duchess of Kent, was related to Alexandra by blood as well as style. She could look exquisite in a beret and a jumper and skirt, too, but official duties demanded more formal dress and she became famous for her hats from the moment of her engagement. Not as relaxed in front of a camera as Alexandra had been, she responded better to people than to lenses.

was a triumph of youthfulness to make the choker, so long associated with dowagers and lorgnettes, seem fresh and fashionable again, but Marina achieved it.

Unlike Alexandra, she devotedly supported British fashion, buying Molyneux (who had Parisian chic and a Paris shop, so perfectly understood his client's continental taste) and, later, Hartnell. This time the fashion magazines and newspapers did not let slip the chance to promote a royal fashion leader and her country's clothes. The Princess's trousseau appeared in full description in *Vogue* before her wedding; she was constantly co-operative with the press which pursued her, especially its quality side. 'Royalty,' as Edna W. Chase, by then Editor-in-Chief of the *Vogue* group, pointed out, 'is scrupulous in the distribution of its favour to the Press, yet, being human, tends to look with amiability on those publications presenting it at its skilfully retouched best.'

Almost as hunted by the fashion press was another lady as at home on the racecourse or on the moors as in Bond Street or on Fifth Avenue. Lady Louis Mountbatten was not lost without her hairdresser, though she was one of the women most keenly watched by fashion writers as a guide to which of the many trends begun by designers or circumstances would be accepted by Society. In January 1930, for example, *Tatler* noted a significant introduction at a Christmas party: 'Lady Louis wore a beaded white frock with a coat to match, which she kept on all the evening, even when she was dancing. These evening coats, first designed for the cold country houses of our more spartan friends, have become a habit and a necessity.' But Lady Louis could happily abandon the world of fashion to shift as it might without her, as she did in 1934 when she set off to ride through the Andes in a pair of old jodhpurs.

Her rôle as a fashion leader had been assigned to her rather than sought. As the sole heiress to a banking fortune ('Miss Ashley has the reputation of owning a dress allowance that runs into four figures,' breathed the *Sketch* when she 'came out' in 1920 in an appropriately golden gown) she would have had to have been quite exceptionally ugly to have avoided it. Since she was slim and blonde, with a clear skin and a decisive taste in clothes, the effect of her choices of costume and accessory was powerful. Through a combination of this accident of fortune and one of nature (she was short-sighted), she even helped to make the magazines realise that horn-rimmed spectacles could be beautiful, which must have been an encouraging discovery for all the downtrodden typists of the '20s and '30s. Though she could dazzle when she wished to, she was not above the frivolous: in the '20s she was known for her very high heels (she had, of course, a very high husband and was only of medium height herself). Yet she disliked the bitty, witty style of the cocktail circuit. Her preference was for the plain and even for the workman-like, in her case represented by a slim tailored suit for day, worn with pearls, gloves and a confident stride. In contrast to Lady Curzon, she did not make much of the opportunities for splendour her time as Vicereine of India gave her.

Edwina Mountbatten, like Princess Marina, looked both relaxed and competent in uniform. At the end of the '30s there was plenty of opportunity to see whose style survived that leveller. The usual fault of the stylised lady in uniform was to look too much like a tailor's dummy: slovenliness was not an error she was capable of. In fact, the simplicity and similarity of fashionable clothes in the period gave them many of the characteristics of uniform. Fashion regulations were depressingly rigid, and hem-lengths were given to the inch in fashion columns. In November 1930 *Tatler* ran down the latest figures – two inches below the knee for sports suits, four inches for tailor-mades, six to eight inches for afternoon dresses. A tape measure was as essential as a long mirror to those who aspired to fashion. As a result of the conformity it is as easy to identify the tidy and the rich in a group of debutantes as it is in a picture of uniformed schoolgirls: by fit, by polish, by posture and carriage of head. It is this factor which explains the apparent paradox that, in a period when individuality was not a quality sought in dress, individuals were immensely influential on fashion.

In group pictures of debutantes at the beginning of the 1930s, one face stands out. Margaret Whigham fixes the photographer with a menacing look from beneath a pair of well-marked eyebrows and dominates the photograph. The determination and ambition are as striking as her beauty. With full face as photogenic as her profile, a small straight nose, beautifully defined lips, creamy skin and a candle-slim body, she did not need to work for compliments or for attention. Yet she seems to have laboured without pause at the task of being the most striking debutante of her generation: an entirely new type.

Where the conventional debutante charmed by her shy appeal, her diffidence, her naturalness, Margaret Whigham mesmerised by her sophistication, her poise and her subtle artificiality. Her carefully-applied make-up, which darkened her lips and shadowed those curiously challenging grey eyes, made her at twenty look an experienced ten years older. When Loelia Ponsonby came out immediately after the

Round the Town

Faces Seen
By Molly Bishop

64 Most mentioned in gossip columns in the early 1930s, debutante of her year, Margaret Whigham, later Mrs Charles Sweeny and later still Duchess of Argyll, brought the sparkling sophistication of the American debutante to London. Her professionalism in dress and with the press was unmatched by anyone of her age. She was chiefly known by her hats, her eyebrows and her dark-painted cupid mouth.

Great War, she found, as many had before her, that the British debutante, accustomed to having had her vanity reproved and her wardrobe scrimped on throughout her schoolgirl years, was ill-equipped to develop dress sense and light conversation overnight when her family suddenly invested in a wardrobe for her at eighteen and pushed her out to attract a rich young man. Margaret Whigham was British, but she spent much of her childhood in New York, where she had seen the sophistication of young American girls and absorbed the

65 Margaret Whigham on a visit to Hartnell, just before her wedding: the press had obviously been forewarned of the time of her appointment. Margaret effortlessly eclipses her two friends, partly by a pose which shows her slim figure to best advantage, partly because she is more neatly and better dressed, but also because she is prettier and determined that this should be recognised: her companion's attempt at a Whigham cool stare is a blank failure.

special freshness and highly-groomed finish of the New World. Her mother allowed her only daughter to indulge her vanity. She had her first perm, to her delight, at the age of eight. When the family returned to England in 1926, Margaret 'slipped out' early. As a schoolgirl she was already dining illicitly in satin and pearls with Etonians in London restaurants, dancing with handsome Argentinians on family holidays in St Moritz and wearing make-up and nail varnish.

It was not surprising that when she finally came out officially, in 1930, she made the other debutantes seem dowdy. She proceeded to smash traditions. According to the *Bystander* she was the first debutante to break away from a snowy, demure coming-out dress; Margaret wore turquoise tulle by a new designer she had faith in, Norman Hartnell. She wore make-up and nail polish brazenly (including luminous pearl-coloured varnish at night); she was the first unmarried girl to be allowed to be a member of the Embassy, the night-club where affairs were conducted with civilised openness by the Prince of Wales and Luigi, the head waiter, was careful to seat couples well away from their marriage partners. 'In fact, she showed the young men on the dance list why debutantes in America have such a good time,' approved the *Bystander*'s gossip columnist – who, like the other gossip writers of the period, was a personal friend of hers.

With notoriety, beauty and constant publicity, it was inevitable that Margaret Whigham's influence should be felt not only on young girls of good family, but on those in the great world outside Mayfair. Lookalikes could be seen in the crowd which massed on the day of her wedding to Charles Sweeny. The dark painted lips, the flirtatious hat tipped well down over one eyebrow and the large pearl earrings were the most obviously imitable features of the Margaret Whigham look (even in American Red Cross uniform during the war, she was seen to tip her cap aslant). If there was a characteristic of her style other than these, it was a tendency to be a trifle ostentatious: although at five feet five inches she could not wear frills, she would wear a little too much beading to a dress, too large a fur, one accessory too many. But beyond this she followed devotedly the tenets of the Long Mirror philosophy. The first of these principles was that no one item should be allowed to dominate another, and the total effect should always be subordinate to its wearer. Margaret Whigham, because of that stern stare of hers and her exceptionally pretty, heart-shaped face, was able to wear hats which would obliterate or make ridiculous most other women. It was exactly the type of infuriating fashion lead which the best excelled at.

Equally important was the rule that everything must co-ordinate precisely. Gloves, bags and shoes must match, and no dress could be worn without the ideal accessories. It was essential to be ruthless on this point, and it meant that a wardrobe had to be highly organised. Not only must everything have its appropriate team to be worn with it, but nothing which was rubbed, soiled or weary-looking was allowed to stay in the wardrobe. Every six months maid and mistress sorted through to see what should be removed and what must be replaced. Everything which remained was expected to work for its hanging space.

The lady's appearance mattered almost more to the maid than to herself. Her chances of a new and better job lay in her reputation. Rosa Lewis, maid in the '20s to Lady Cranborne, recalled, 'She was a great credit to me . . . ladies' maids were very much judged by the way their employers were dressed.' It was an incentive to watch not only the condition of the clothes, but where and when her mistress wore them. A good maid could warn her lady that she had worn an outfit in a resort or country house before. This did not mean that it was essential to have a new dress for every occasion, though. On the contrary: buying for a special event suggested that there were few of them in your life and was considered common. A lady knew what her social calendar would demand of her and bought her wardrobe with that in mind. Hardy Amies remembers that it was the women who were least used to racing who bought a whole new set of outfits for Ascot. The true racing women had clothes which were correct already, which they wore throughout the season.

Lastly, it was important to follow shifts in fashion. An inch change in hemlines could result in the dowdiness of the unprepared. The collections were part of the season's social round, like Hurlingham or Wimbledon. Even those who did not buy would pick up hints. Rosa Lewis and Lady Cranborne can not have been the only tandem of mistress and maid silently memorising details of French frocks so that they could be re-created more cheaply at home. Margaret Whigham, or Mrs Charles Sweeny as she became, cleverly bought smart day dresses in America, where they were well-priced and well-cut, and went to France for evening wear.

All this required its considerable sacrifice of time. Despite the new age of machines and modernity, a woman might still change five times a day, and three changes were common. Besides the shopping and hours of fittings which were usual in Alexandra's day there was a new burden added: the demands of the hair, face and figure. Wallis used to keep the Duke of Windsor flicking through the magazines while the hairdressers laboured over her. New, refined techniques of perming and colouring replaced the hours spent brushing and pinning, despite the supposedly easy short cuts available to the modern woman. And this was the golden age of the beauty salon, when a weekly manicure was only basic grooming and a woman of style could spend hours having unwanted hair removed, existing hair dyed, eyebrows plucked (Wallis destroyed a fine pair of strong American eyebrows which accentuated her best feature, her blue, intense eyes), their skins squeezed clean and their blemishes removed by knife and needle. The most desired and exclusive beauty routine of the late 1930s was that of Dr Erno Laszlo, used by both Wallis and Greta Garbo. A complicated system of many

66 Daisy, Mrs Reginald Fellowes, in about 1930, dressed with apparent carelessness in a little plain top and a short plain skirt with a beret, but tense with effort of looking perfectly natural.

steps, designed to cherish the skin like a daily facial, it was not intended for the working woman with but a few moments to spare in the morning. Dr Laszlo's prescription for the average skin included a morning cleanse with thirty rinses in very hot water. It was a ritual of purification, and it took the devotee's time.

The body, in its poses and postures, had also to be restrained. There was a deliberate quality about the stylised lady's movements which reflected time spent studying their effect. There was no slumping, even amongst the most casually dressed. Daisy Fellowes, heiress to the Singer fortune, notorious for breaking hearts and for her ability to make every woman in a room feel overdressed on her entrance, stares confidently into camera lenses apparently relaxed – but every limb is tense in the posture of effortless elegance. The backs of these women were straight, their walks studied. One of the Prince of Wales's first impressions of Mrs Simpson was that she had 'grace of carriage and natural dignity of movement', but she betrays tension in every picture – the more as her sartorial responsibilities increase.

Small everyday gestures, like the smoking of a cigarette or the lighting of it, were done with an air. Perhaps the most characteristic gesture of the stylised lady of the '30s was the way in which she publicly made up. Enamelled and even jewelled powder compacts were made as props to this small theatrical performance. The compact was lifted proudly to a level with the eyes, gazed into intently with the concentration of a picture restorer about to begin work on a masterpiece, and lipstick or powder was applied with an unhurried care which excluded any viewers from the performer's notice. Once done, the compact was snapped shut and the beauty returned to conversation with her audience.

During the early 1920s debutantes still did not admit, except to their intimates, the use of a little lip-salve or a touch of rouge. One mother, according to Loelia Ponsonby, advised her daughter to touch her nose up with soap if it shone. To make up in public was a provocative act even in 1930, especially for a debutante, but it was the stylised beauty's declaration of blatant artificiality. Sweet naturalness, so valued by the Edwardians, when natural assets like curly hair and a clear skin made the beauties stand out in their generation, was outmoded.

Because of this, and because success at the Long Mirror Look was chiefly a question of keeping closely to the rules, it was less than ever necessary for a leader of fashion to be pretty. Ambition and determination mattered more: the two qualities that Wallis Simpson and Gertrude Lawrence appeared to have in common. Clapham-reared and far from beautiful, Gertrude Lawrence played the fantasy figure of the sophisticated woman when in 1930 *Private Lives* opened in London with her in the starring role of Amanda. Brittle, witty and beautifully dressed, in a series of satin dressing-robes and shimmering gowns, Amanda was copied by audiences and designers in London and in New York in 1931. So that Gertrude's wardrobe would always look pristine, it was replaced every six weeks by identical new garments.

Gertrude's career as a leader of fashion had started when she was a child with the realisation, as she watched her actress mother pad her tights with cotton wool for a pantomime part, 'that frequently a woman's legs (and not her face) are her fortune'. Gertrude's legs were good, her blue eyes were pretty (though set too wide apart) and she had good hands. Apart from these assets, she had little in her favour: a large mouth shaped something like a boomerang, a lumpy face, a prominent Adam's apple and a dominating nose. Charm and vitality were what helped transform Gertrude into an object of women's envy and men's pursuit, added to a 'Gentlemen Prefer Blondes' brand of naive ambition

67 Not a beauty, but a creature of entirely self-created glamour, Gertrude Lawrence worked ceaselessly at her own image. Casual elegance, on and off stage, was her achievement; she never looked as though she tried too hard. The scarf at the neck and the cigarette in long holder in her hand are two familiar mannerisms, but the pose, with one hip thrown slightly out of line and a faint air of boredom, is the most characteristic part of the ensemble.

and ruthlessness. She had from an early age an actress's ability to charm by movement. Her walk was a delight to watch, her smile was sparkling, her gestures perfectly controlled. The ability to use make-up to enhance her appearance was a matter of professional competence. Gertie sensibly outlined her lips a little within their natural fullness and attempted to widen her eyes with long false eyelashes, and less sensibly at one point dispensed with her eyebrows altogether, drawing them a quarter of an inch above their natural place to give a curiously clown-like effect.

Society's tricks of speech and dress she learnt as mistress of Captain Philip Astley, whom she met while working in Murray's night-club immediately after the First World War. In the Household Cavalry, he was rich, sophisticated and happy to play Professor Higgins to an able pupil. So quick to learn was she, indeed, that Gertrude was soon welcomed into the most exclusive quarters, including the Prince of

Wales's bedroom. 'There was just a narrow, single bed with a table beside it on which there was often,' she wrote significantly in her autobiography, 'a glass of milk and an apple.'

Norman Hartnell, who dressed her for the stage, as did Molyneux, testified to her extraordinary ability to wear clothes. She acted the best out of them, becoming languorous in satin sheaths and pearls, chirpy and witty in afternoon suits with their characteristic spotted-bow-necked blouses, whirling and flirtatious in full-skirted ball gowns. Like Vivien Leigh, she could flatter the dresses she wore, and be relied on never to be slip-shod about accessories. On-stage she sometimes took more trouble over her clothes than the parts she played, according to those who worked with her later, and off-stage she was just as meticulous in her everyday rôle as star. She never stopped acting. Life was a series of spotted silk pyjamas (silk pyjamas and satin dressing-gowns seem to have played much the same part in the life of the 1930s seductress as the tea gown had in the 1880s) and glamorous affairs.

The stylised lady's interior design, like her clothes, has a designer label, is orderly, gleaming and in a colour which flatters her complexion. Mrs Simpson liked her favourite blue for walls, or blush colour; Gertrude Lawrence chose Sybil Colefax to create her a white, mirrored drawing room, to reflect her image and her usual deep suntan. Her rooms, like herself, were freshly scented each day, each to match a different mood. There was Chanel No. 5 for the dining room, with its sparkling silver-sequinned curtains, and Dans la Nuit by Worth for the bedroom.

Not only had Gertrude mastered the flamboyant style of the star, she was so confident of her ability to play the Society lady that she could invert her snobbery. In her dining room guests might be served amusing Cockney dishes – bloaters, for example, with mustard sauce – and she could carry a casual air well in her clothes, throwing a mink over a pair of grey flannels or wearing a beret to dine at Grosvenor House.

Mrs Simpson's rise was not from so low a starting point, but it was faster, further and just as triumphant. On her arrival in London she was both dowdy and plain, for the future Duchess of Windsor's much-remarked-on flair for dress was painfully and slowly acquired. Amusing, with a pair of bright eyes and a reasonably slim figure, she had a certain sparkle in conversation, but no prettiness. Margaret Whigham thought that her skirts were too long, and that the ear-muff style in which she wore her hair was desperately dull. Cecil Beaton found her 'brawny and raw-boned'. Lady Furness, who introduced her to the Prince of Wales, saw no threat. Her voice was raucous, her round face bore some resemblance to Mary Poppins' (she was noticed to nanny the King on later occasions) and even her hands were ugly. She was in her mid-thirties and she was only five feet four inches tall. Yet within three and a half years of her first meeting with the Prince she had removed him from Thelma's care, and by the beginning of the Second World War she was sharing top place in the list of best-dressed women in the world with Princess Marina. It was a case of the frog being kissed by the Prince.

From the beginning, Wallis was in close contact with the impeccable Thelma Furness, who not only befriended her and invited her to regular parties, but in 1931 lent her her own feathers and train for her court presentation. By then the ear-muffs had been replaced by a sleek, shining hair-do which was strongly reminiscent of Thelma's own, waving close down her face from a central parting. Thelma's dress sense was not absorbed so quickly. Not until after Thelma's displacement did Lady Mendl attempt to take Wallis's wardrobe in hand and point her to the better couturiers. When in 1935 the gossip columnists began to feature this unknown as a fashion leader, her style was still far from its final polish. The photographs did little to explain to surprised readers why Mrs Simpson deserved the sudden accolades: they showed an immensely happy-looking, middle-aged woman smiling at the cameras with a grin which broadened her nose and made her eyes look smaller. What was written in the magazines' fashion columns only made the problem more mysterious. On 12 June 1935 the *Bystander* showed a sketch of Wallis in a small hat, captioning it airily, 'A Sketch of the attractive American made at the Ritz's crowded lunch time. She was wearing her famous blue ermine cape, and a little blue hat with a feather and an eye veil.' Famous for what, readers must have wondered, though the inner circles did not need to speculate. Queen Mary was later heard to say mournfully of her son, the King, 'He gives Mrs Simpson the most lovely jewels.'

Bright blue, far too hard a shade for her, was still Wallis's favourite colour (once she was Duchess of Windsor, couturiers persuaded her into mid-blue shades, or deep purple-blues which flattered her better) and she still made other bad mistakes of taste. Her penchant for little-girl clothes horrified Diana Cooper, who saw her in a baby's bonnet on the 1936 cruise on the *Nahlin* and found the contrast between it and the adult face inside both absurd and grotesque. But there was a difference since her early days in London: she had grown in confidence. Cecil Beaton re-met and re-assessed her, and concluded that she was as improved in dress as in social connections. She had lost weight (her dinner party accounts of her diets riveted the King) so her face was less chubby and her figure had more distinction. She began to smile less often for cameras and to order her wardrobe from Schiaparelli. Her elegance was being gradually created. With the news of the abdication crisis, the *Bystander* ran a spread of photographs of Wallis, including one of her at a reception, cleverly dressed in an oriental-looking brocade top which brought out the Chinese doll-like qualities in her face, sandals, and a straight velvet skirt. 'As usual,' ran the caption, 'she was beautifully dressed and supremely soignée. Everyone who knows her is agreed on her flair for dress.' From then on she grew ever more thin and independent. On the eve of her wedding she changed from her Thelma Furness style of hair to a new one, with the waves running up from her face and lightening it a little. Where brides of British royalty by tradition wore British-made dresses, the new American Duchess defiantly wore the American Mainbocher then and afterwards. Her looks improved with age and cosmetic surgery, she acquired dignity in front of the cameras and a photogenic smile. There were no more lapses. The dresses she bought from Mainbocher, then Balenciaga, Dior, Déssès and de Givenchy were severely plain, set off only by hours of grooming spent in beauty salons and hairdressers, by a 34-24-34 figure ('Dachau thin', according to Diana Cooper) and by her splendid jewels.

Yet despite its apparent simplicity, this was a style of very conspicuous consumption. Good fit and cut and cloth are the almost inimitable virtues of the best couture, and they are most evident in simple clothes, whereas in elaborate frocks poor quality can be to some extent disguised by ornament. Women who led fashion in this period were usually very rich: Margaret Whigham's father had a fortune made in the development of Celanese, Thelma Furness was married to a millionaire, and the woman most famous for a style of dressing stripped of ornament, Daisy Fellowes, inherited the Singer fortune. She might be seen in the Baccarat Room at Cannes in the simplest of dark blue suits and a matching beret, but it was an example lesser and poorer women would be unwise to follow. It would be the best of all possible simple navy suits, but its effectiveness was chiefly as a setting for a characterful and confident face, with a wry smile and large, attentively intelligent eyes. Hands in pockets, chin held high, Daisy Fellowes could dominate a room with apparent carelessness. Like Margaret

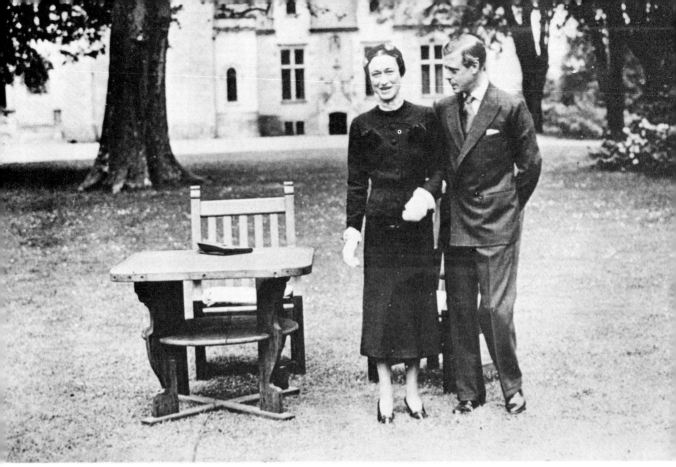

68 (above) A 1937 engagement picture of Mrs
Simpson at the Château de Chande betrays that
a certain naïveté has not left her. She has not
quite learnt how to smile for the camera without
losing her eyes, nor that her centre parting looks
painfully pulled. But she is already obsessively
thin and neat, a great improvement on her past,
undistinguished appearance before she
became an intimate of the Prince's.

69 The now-confident Duchess of Windsor in
1953, at a gala ball at Versailles. Wallis has
learnt how to smile only with her mouth and
teeth, how to pose to take best advantage of a
reportage photograph, and to soften her
hair-style. Few women improve with age but
Wallis, with a combination of hard work and
money available to spend at the best couturiers
and beauty salons, was able to do so: she
claimed it was her duty to her husband. She was
addicted to modern jewellery – but not to false.

153

Whigham's hats, her clothes gave a fashion lead which it was almost impossible for other women to follow.

Stylised dressers liked the hard glitter of metal, and appreciated that against a plain background jewellery is at its most impressive. Their jewellery was large and usually modern, a demonstration of present wealth rather than past family fame. Not for them the heirloom fenders of obedient wives or antique jewellery worn, like Ottoline Morrell's, for its nostalgic associations with a richer past; old jewellery was best re-made and re-set. It was firmly subordinated to its wearer and matched as carefully as shoes and handbag were. Cecil Beaton recounts how Margaret Whigham, then the Duchess of Argyll, pointed out another woman's deficiencies at dinner on a transatlantic liner in 1955: 'Oh, do look at Lady Rosse with amber necklace and diamond bracelets and sapphire brooch. Oh dear, she hasn't thought that parure out!'

This perfectionism meant that it was necessary to own quite a lot of jewellery for different occasions and outfits, though not as much as Gertrude Lawrence, who when she bankrupted herself through extravagance in 1935, had £16,000 of rocks in pawn. Even their dogs had expensive, pedigree labels. The correct canine accessory had been a matter of fashion for years: in 1914 dogs featured as frequently on the pages of *Vogue* as handbags or gloves, and in as many sizes, shapes and colours to suit their mistresses' appearance. The more remote-sounding breeds were favoured: Lhasa terriers, Salukis, Happas, Pyrenean mountain dogs and the fashionably ugly Brussels griffon. Just in case a reader might suppose the *Vogue* editor had a personal passion for dogs, an article on 15 March 1914, unequivocally headed 'How Fashion Fashions Dogs', explained, 'The Modern Dog is not Required to Feel or Think; He must Only Look, – Look His Pedigree, His Cost, and His Part in His Mistress's costume.' Margaret Whigham favoured black poodles (good dogs for fastidious dressers, leaving no hairs), the Duchess of Windsor cairn terriers, and Gertrude Lawrence a black miniature schnautzer.

The clothes of the stylised dresser had designer labels as a matter of course, or were copied from designer's inventions. She was not concerned with originality in her garments; not for her the little woman who could run up something to her own idea. Her great respect for professionalism meant that she was happy to leave the business of dress designing to experts, though she had an eye for cut and quality and could bargain shrewdly over price. The more extraordinary fancies of the designer's brain would be avoided. A degree of wit in dressing – a

Schiaparelli print of two interlocked lobsters, or a hat veil with a crossed kiss on it to fall over the cheek – was acceptable, the eccentric was not. But although the best-dressed women did not allow any designer to foist a garment on them which would not fit their own unalterable style, they were surprisingly willing to experiment to discover what new fashions might fit that style. The Duchess of Windsor tried hot pants in the 1960s, though worn with a skirt, and Margaret, Duchess of Argyll, in the early 1980s found to her surprise that she could wear knee-breeches.

The stylist's own professionalism came in looking after her face and figure and her ability to put a look together. In the 1930s she was still more important than her designer: the label was worn on the inside. Though '90s men like George Cornwallis-West complained that after the Great War the Royal Enclosure at Ascot was full of journalists and hairdressers, the dress-designer was still not certain, when visiting a client, whether he would be taken through the tradesmen's entrance or the front door. In gossip columns frocks were described with the name of the wearer, not the designer, and it was regarded as a small triumph for the designer to have won his client a mention. Corisande, in the *Evening Standard*, ran regular reviews of what Society was wearing and what fashions it was creating, alongside less glamorous descriptions of what was in the shops. 'Outsize Bows Were Worn at Newmarket' ran a typical headline. At the Big Ben Ball at Grosvenor House, 'One of the loveliest dresses was worn by Lady Scone. It was of white stiffened chiffon. Great waterlilies, made of swan's feathers, were round the shoulders and to catch the frills of the skirt,' rhapsodised Corisande on 10 March 1934. If there were strong pressures not to wear the same dress twice before Corisande's keen eyes, there were also benefits to the beauty's budget from such publicity. Free dresses were given to women like Lady Diana Cooper in return for it. Society and the fashion trade – and the media – were growing closer. Mrs Worthington might put her daughter on the catwalk as well as the stage by now, for in 1930 the trend for young Society girls to work as models was relatively new. Photographs of Society beauties were no longer sold in corner shops, but they could be bought in magazines and they were often wearing borrowed clothes for the purpose of advertisement, though of the softest-selling kind. Dorothy Wilding, Society photographer of the '20s and '30s, photographed 'hat models for a Mr O'Connor, who owned the Condor Hat Company. Society women and leading actresses would come along to be photographed in a Condor hat, and the pictures I made would eventually find their way into the best magazines. The whole operation was an example of the kind of promotion work already commencing in those days in the West End of London.'

Wilding's photographs were popular with magazines because they had a saccharine sweetness which was entirely divorced from reality. She spent a year learning the art of retouching before launching herself as a photographer, and she put her skill to maximum use. It was necessary not only to flatter the photographed subject but for the sake of the magazines and trade, in whose best interest it was, to create an image of a Society of beautiful, expensively-clothed women. It stimulated demand in the mass market, but it was not easy in the age of photography. Shots taken outside at county events revealed to the public that duchesses and ladies frequently looked dishevelled and fat. When a Society woman appeared, like Diana Manners or Margaret Whigham, who resembled the ideal, she could claim all the publicity and treats she wanted.

The stylised beauties of the '30s were as professional about publicity as about their wardrobes. The camera was for them an extension of their looking-glass. Margaret Whigham was as charming to journalists as to her hosts, and a reliable source of good pictures from the moment of her coming out, which was previewed in the press. Even on her way to her presentation at the Palace, dressed like every other debutante in regulation dress, it was Margaret Whigham who was photographed in the queue of Rolls and Bentleys, her door co-operatively open, coolly stitching at a piece of fine needlework to while away the time.

Mrs Simpson also cultivated her links with the press, notably the stylist's text-book, *Vogue*. Her link was the Californian writer John McMullin, to whom, before the abdication, she not only released sketches of her new season's wardrobe but on whose behalf she pestered the King after his father's death for a good commemorative picture.

But even with such mutually helpful co-operation, Society stylists were not quite satisfactory enough as promoters to the masses of fashion. Divorced from their surroundings and their circles, their dress sense is less impressive. Even the svelte Daisy Fellowes's photograph looked disappointing to the average reader who hoped for obvious and copiable leads. The most influential women in the 1930s were those who had least control over their own images: the movie stars. Painted, dressed, packaged, lit and retouched in the interest of their studios and profit, their style had nothing to do with real life. Ted Allen, stills photographer for the stars, remembered photographing Jean Harlow at

70 Convent-neat, schoolgirl-
fresh, Vivien Leigh seemed, in
1938 when this picture was
taken, to have scooped every
desirable commodity including
beauty, Laurence Olivier and
dress sense. Off-screen or off-
stage, her early style was crisp
and simple. She was a joy for
designers to dress because
she acted the best out of any
garment, which her looks in
any case enhanced. As she
grew older her taste for
simplicity, like everything else,
disintegrated.

a time when the moguls decided that she should change her blonde
bombshell image: 'They told me to make a lady of her. The hairdresser
darkened her hair. She didn't object to it. She figured the powers that be
must know.' Women across the world wondered why, with imitated
make-up and similar hair-styles, they still did not look like their screen
goddesses. The reason was simply that the goddesses did not look like
that, either. After the next war the lead of the individual in fashion was
to be handed over almost entirely to professional, manipulated, artificial
leaders of style who displayed very little of their own individuality in
their dress.

8

The Princess and the Punk

'Faces, my children, have gone completely out of fashion, they are no longer worn.' The sibyl pronouncer was Edith Sitwell, the date 1965, when her autobiography, *Taken Care Of*, was published. Faces as unusual as hers, as she was well aware, had not been in fashion for some centuries, but the look considered beautiful in the 1960s was particularly artificial and robot-like: big-eyed, pale-mouthed, childishly unmarked by time or personality.

Besides the faces of the film stars, the faces prominent in the 1950s and 1960s were those of professional beauties, the models who looked lovely for a living. In the 1950s the models could make marriages into titles as impressive as those made by actresses at the beginning of the century: Fiona Campbell Walter married Baron von Thyssen and Bronwen Pugh, Balmain's favourite model, married Lord Astor. But though models like these, Barbara Goalen and later Twiggy and Shrimp were famous names, the fame came not from their style in their private lives but from the way they looked in front of a camera – a look which was chiefly the invention of other people. It had become usual at photo sessions, especially for the magazines, where reproduction is better than in newspapers and details can be better seen, for a whole team of experts to be assembled, in much the same way as they had been for stills shots of film stars in the '30s. The make-up artist, especially for colour photographs, took over some of the jobs of the retoucher. More sophisticated products and improved techniques of application could transform a poor skin into one which looked flawless, disguise shadows and wrinkles and give an unnaturally healthy glow to pale cheeks, but the effect was artificial and far removed from what was suitable for the street, away from bright studio lighting. In the mid-1970s, models over whom the make-up artist had laboured for an hour would carefully cleanse and lightly re-make up their faces to leave, for fear of being stared at in the outside world. Nevertheless, magazines, eager to please the big advertisers among the beauty product companies, listed by

71 & 72 There are two sides to every fashion model, but one is rarely seen. Clive Arrowsmith's pictures for the *Sunday Times Magazine* in 1982 highlight the artificiality of studio fashion photography. But even this is an exercise in studio artificiality, and to make the point it has been exaggerated beyond the bounds of reality. The model's head rarely needs to be clipped into position!

159

their photographs every kind of product used, as though they were essential to the would-be-beautiful reader.

The artificiality of this exercise was increased by the fact that it was common practice to credit colours and brands which had not been used on the model. The typical make-up artist's kit consisted of such a mêlée of new and old paints which might be blended together that they were almost impossible to list truthfully. More than that, colours changed with the processes of photography and printing, so that in extreme cases an apricot-coloured lipstick could look bluish in the magazine. Truth was, in the circumstances, only an approximation, and women who went to buy a new eye-shadow, inspired by a glossy photograph, often found themselves disappointed.

Besides the make-up artist there were the hairdresser, the stylist to choose and arrange the clothes, and the photographer; the model's opinion on her look was very rarely sought. The model, who was picked to suit the clothes and not the other way round. They commonly did not fit. A row of bulldog clips down the back of a blouse might ensure the illusion of a fit; double-sided tape would keep a tricky collar lying close to the neck; pins would re-arrange the gathers on a skirt. By the time a creative stylist had worked on the garments they could look quite different. It increased the baffling aura of fantasy and glamour about the magazines, since even the purchase or making up of the identical clothes featured in them could not create the same effect on the woman who had to wear them in normal life and be able not only to move but to be seen from the back.

Though good fashion editors kept the requirements of their readers in mind and steered their photographic teams away from the creative extravagances to which they were prone, there was inevitably a lack of reality in the photographs. Lillie Langtry, and even the picture-postcard actresses, had chosen their own clothes for the stage and applied their own make-up. Modern professional beauties' names were not even given in magazine credits, though fame made the faces of some recognisable. A few had out-of-studio and off-catwalk careers which received something approaching Lillie's publicity: Jerry Hall, whose status as Mick Jagger's official lover made her international gossip column material, expressed an opinion which might have been an echo of Lillie's when she claimed, in an interview for *Tatler* in October 1982, that, after sex, what she desired most were 'giant sapphires, emeralds and rubies'. Her off-stage clothes, in Jagger's company at least, appeared to be in the tradition of the mistress: blatantly sexy, designer-made and

160

73 Professional beauty Jerry Hall in a familiar paradox, slipping out of a back entrance to avoid publicity yet surrounded by cameras. No-one looks surprised. He is in ramshackle casual clothes; she, possessively clutched, is in full make-up, diamonds, pearls and a frivolous little number which suggests that just at the moment she does not wish to be taken too seriously. Professional Beauty dressing has not changed much since the days of Mary Cornwallis-West and her ptarmigan hat (see page 33).

in the dizziest blonde heights of fashion. But she was an exception in the 1970s, when models were more likely to appear outside the studios in jeans and old clothes, so dishevelled and bare of make-up that strangers would find it hard to believe their occupation.

Though seen from the back, and therefore dressed without the help of bulldog clips, the models of the catwalk at the designer shows (especially in Paris and Milan) were almost as distant from the real world as those in photographs. With the admittance of press and photographers to the fashion presentations, the designers began to compete for attention by producing theatrical shows. The make-up was theatrically strong, the accessorising done to exaggerate the new feature of a look rather than suggest to buyers what should be worn with the clothes: in 1979, for example, with the wide-shouldered look of the '40s, Jap caricatured a military air with a plumed Ruritarian cap complete with chin-strap.

161

Many of the garments were designed for no purpose other than to startle: moulded plastic breastplates, for example, which had few uses in anyone's social round.

For designers after the Second World War were the accepted and unrivalled lords of fashion. There was no equivalent of the Empress Eugénie to help a Dior's fame when he introduced the New Look in 1947, and he did not appear to suffer from her absence. The social position of designers soared, and by the 1960s they formed part of the party set in their own right. Magazines were filled with their opinions on dress and its philosophy. Words like 'King' (of Dior) and 'Dauphin' (of St Laurent) were employed to describe them, perhaps because there were few real kings left and little of the aristocratic social rounds they once made glorious. The great country houses of Britain were becoming fewer each year, abandoned because of the smell of the drains or the cost of servants or the ravages of death duties. Laundresses skilled in the use of the goffering iron and starching found themselves unwanted. Young girls in country villages no longer aspired to the life of travel and finery which was that of the lady's maid, and more ladies followed Daisy Fellowes's example and learnt to wash their own stockings. There were fewer places to go when all dressed up, at least in couture clothes: 'the season' was in its death-throes. Although the young Queen of England was young and attractive, she was besotted not by clothes but by racehorses. Formal evening dress was for her working dress: rather than from her own style, she continued to patronise her mother's favourite house, Hartnell, and was of surprisingly little value as a promoter of her country's fashion abroad. In 1957 she stopped court presentations, and of the shreds of the old Society calendar left, Ascot seemed in best shape.

There were a few stars of couture left. Audrey Hepburn's quirky, lively face gave the dark, tight, perfectly-fitting dresses she wore a youthful glamour in the 1950s, and in the very early '60s a young and lovely woman occupied by chance one of the positions which gave a most traditional opportunity to lead fashion: that of the wife of the highest official in a republic. Jacqueline Kennedy was perfectly fitted by background, interests and looks to lead American fashion and play the part of the beautiful and good wife of the Golden Boy president. Ten years before, she had produced enough surface sophistication to win American *Vogue*'s talent contest. She was passionately interested in clothes. She was at ease in American society, her father was a rich stockbroker, she was as happy on horseback as in the ballroom, and

162

74 Jackie Kennedy, looking beautiful and good, and remarkably like a doll, in London in 1962. Neat, natural and simply dressed, she is the model for many a housewife: she looks chic, but not sharp.

even her lady's maid, Providentia, had an ante-bellum ring to her name. Jackie's innocent-looking face, with its huge dark eyes, fresh skin and wide, delighted smile, was a gift to any President's propaganda and publicity machine.

Once that machine had directed her away from Paris and made her buy American couture (she patronised Oleg Cassini, but she frequently imposed her own taste on him, sending him sketches of her own to work from) she was its greatest saleswoman, aided by the new medium of television. News programmes showed her wardrobe day by day, and it was a look which was particularly imitable: ideal dress for the ideal wife who hoped to help her husband's career along. In its cheaper versions, it was as relevant to a salesman's wife as a President's. Like Princess Alexandra a century before, Jacqueline chose for day wear neat, sweet suits. They were simple, immaculate, fitted exactly, and

163

were matched by unassuming accessories – hat, gloves and shoes in conservatively classic shapes. It was up-to-date, but it eschewed the extravagance and whimsy of high fashion, and it had nothing to do with the hard-edged smartness of the 1930s.

The stars of that past period were unimpressed by the Kennedy style. Cecil Beaton thought she had shoulders like a baseball player and an incipient moustache. Not only did Jackie not dress in sharply chic clothes in public, she was determinedly casual in private, appearing before the startled White House staff, used to First Ladies thirty years her senior, in trousers and with tousled hair. Glittering cocktail parties, the stylised woman's favourite display case, were abandoned in favour of a more traditional type of entertainment: black-tie dinners, for which the First Lady wore impressive and complicated gowns from which her maid had to un-hook her at the end of the evening.

Had she been Queen Consort instead of President's wife, it would have been a promising start to a reign as fashion leader in which she might have ended as dictator. As it was, she was closely copied in the States and abroad, but the disadvantages to fashion of a republic rather than a kingdom had not altered fundamentally since October 1875, when the satirical *World* had run an interview with an unnamed Paris couturier on 'Who Starts The Fashion?' ' "Dressing the world," he said, "was the simplest of all matters when we had a monarchy in France. You dressed the Queen or Empress, and your task was done. I am no politician, but depend upon it the present state of things cannot last. We have no supreme person to wear our clothes. It is astonishing to me that they have over-looked that."

' "The President's wife," I ventured to suggest.

' "A President's wife," he replied, "does not represent stability, permanence. She is here to-day and gone tomorrow. She guarantees no continuity of individual taste. The result – they have never originated a fashion in America. It is the prime defect of their four-years term. They are trying to alter it, as you see, by electing for second terms. . . . But it won't do. You have hardly time to study a woman's character, much less learn her shape, in seven or eight years." '

Jacqueline Kennedy's time with the glamour of the White House to back her style was tragically shorter than most. Though she continued to be photographed and copied, her power, without her title, was much reduced. It was a great loss to couture, which by the mid-1960s seemed old and frumpish, strictly for the face-lift age group – and even they were buying less of it. The price of labour had sent the cost of time-consuming couture perfection to such a height that the rich, like the Duchess of Windsor, might be seen in the same dress three years running. In 1968 Balenciaga, the greatest perfectionist amongst his generation of couturiers, closed his business, explaining in an interview a few years later to Prudence Glynn, Fashion Editor of *The Times*, 'The life which supported couture is finished.'

The leaders of the new social life which the papers reported were in the business of entertainment and music. Wives of rock and pop stars, if they wished to take it, had the chance of publicity previously according to Society's duchesses. But few whose income did not depend on looks took the opportunities to flaunt a personal style as eagerly as Bianca Jagger. First seen in the papers as a young, unknown Nicaraguan girl-friend of Michael Caine, in mini-skirt and laddered tights, she had even then a distinctly unusual and feline type of style. At least, that was Mr Caine's opinion: 'She is like,' he was reported as saying, 'a panther cub who is potentially dangerous but who still needs help.' By 1970 the panther cub had moved on to Mick Jagger and was to be seen dressed in the kind of eye-catching disguise – white trouser suit and dark glasses in November – which was the very important person's usual dress at the period in which to be seen avoiding the press. Jackie Kennedy's version was a raincoat, head-scarf and dark glasses, recognisable at airports throughout the world and a much-copied publicity-tease.

Bianca's style in the years which followed could be seen to have an unusual source of inspiration: her husband. The similarity between her mouth and his was much remarked on, but for those who had missed this point Bianca caricatured a boyish look. She irritated her husband by going to the same tailor (Tommy Nutter) as he did. Paraded in night-clubs, with a mannish hat and an antique cane from her collection, this joke transvestitism attracted press attention even when her husband was out of town. It was cleverly contrasted by Bianca's other style, based on her wildcat looks. Dark-eyed, with milky amber skin and very definite cheek-bones, she smouldered (through practice or natural talent) in a series of dresses from Ossie Clark, Zandra Rhodes and St Laurent which fell into two categories: the slinky and the skimpy. At her wedding she wore a St Laurent trouser suit and a see-through blouse.

Not content with looking like a cat, she groomed herself as obsessively. There were weekly manicures and pedicures at which her nails were painted scarlet, and long sessions at the hairdresser, where her hair was steeped in coconut oil and steamed. 'Looking special,' said

75 Slit, sexy, and feline in general effect: Bianca Jagger's personal style comes over despite the wearing of a designer dress which has been boldly signed by the designer, Zandra Rhodes. Bianca managed to look boyish in very seductive and bare dresses, yet girlish in men's suits.

Bianca in 1972, 'is a question of imagination.' She deliberately avoided, she said, the look of a designer, preferring to stamp her own mark on her clothes, and added, unnecessarily, 'I love to dress up.' She was famous, apart from her marriage, purely for her looks and style and was one of the party people whose face would automatically be recorded by any photographer sent to a new night-club, a publicity party or even a private ball. She was on the party list in her own right.

But it was not only at the expensive parties and night-clubs that fashion was worn and made in the 1970s. The usual progress of influence, from the top to the bottom of society, could be reversed. In the last century the adoption of a new style in bonnets by the maid meant that the mistress would discard her own and move on to a mode as yet untainted by a working-class face. In the 1960s boutique clothes, cheaply and widely available, made it easy for any girl to be as up-to-the-minute, if in less well-made clothes, as the richest pop star's wife. A

76 A combination of the banal and the bizarre as sinister and as effective as Nancy Cunard's. Jordan, shop girl turned punk fashion leader, in a twin-set and plain skirt, but with hair and make-up designed to horrify. Both eyebrows are shaved and almost the entire side of the face is painted with a pink bruise. Worn in the film *Jubilee* and on the King's Road thereafter, this look produced an army of punk imitators.

hairdresser or a shop assistant in the fashion capitals was likely to be more fashionably dressed than many of her customers. She might even innovate.

Punk, for example, the '70s style of deliberate ugliness and fake aggression in dress, had its strange equivalent of Lillie Langtry in Jordan. In the mid-1970s she was mobbed on the King's Road, pursued by photographers, copied in make-up and clothes and lionised at parties to which she was invited for the kudos of her presence and the publicity which she attracted. She was the archetype of the punk woman, and she served behind the till at a shop. The shop in question was Sex, where Vivienne Westwood's punk designs were sold, but Jordan was not a house model. She wore punk at its most extreme for every second of her normal life, though her life became increasingly abnormal to match her clothes and as a result of them. Her commuting into work by train from Brighton to London in suspenders, see-through

167

knickers and blouse and white bouffant hair produced so many stares, comments from outraged passengers and questions from curious American tourists that British Rail allowed her to travel in the quieter first-class carriages.

Her exhibitionism had begun early. At fourteen, in 1969, she had surprised the inhabitants of the small seaside town of Seaforth in Sussex by wearing transparent net skirts and suspenders, and she was expelled from school for appearing in the classroom with her hair in a Mohican cut with a red centre and three pink stripes at the back. Her clothes were bought at nearby Brighton, filled with 1960s tat. Work as a shop assistant in Harrods, where she wore a green face, was soon abandoned for more congenial surroundings: the shop Sex, and its punk clothes.

Jordan's most refreshing quality, in a fashion world sated with professional public relations coups, was her amateurism. No model agency would even have interviewed her. She was too short – only five feet one inch – too fat and too plain. Since the whole point of punk was to shock, she was the ideal girl to popularise it amongst the King's Road youth. Her contributions to Vivienne Westwood's clothes were make-up and hairstyles, barbaric and elaborate. Hours of experiment were put in to ensure that the results would be startling enough. A new make-up would be worn for six months and then changed to a different, and if possible more sinister, look. A combination of devilish black, slanting eye make-up, with lines of paint streaking up from the sides of her eyes, and a brush-spiked haircut for which special techniques were evolved, was copied by almost every punk dresser. It was followed by a less imitable by equally off-putting 'Bride of Frankenstein' appearance, for which Jordan wore red contact lenses which covered her entire eyes. Sometimes she achieved a more subtly surreal effect by wearing the respectable and dowdy suits, complete with plastic handbag, of an elderly female Bingo player, with her own punk hair and make-up.

It was not surprising that photographers who heard rumours of a new and news-worthy cult and began their investigations at its centre, Sex, saw Jordan as a good example of the type at its most extreme. Her image, like Langtry's an exact century earlier, appeared everywhere. She was interviewed in the teenage magazines, modelled clothes for fashion photographers and had her photograph, by David Bailey, on the cover of *Ritz*, the insider's fashion magazine. She was invited to star in a punk film, *Jubilee*. Then invitations, from people she did not know to a rich PR party round she was not familiar with, began to fall through her door. Her photograph was taken as often as Bianca's. At first, revelling in it all, she went to every party.

But if the response to a newly fashionable face had not changed much in a hundred years, neither had the frustrations of having more attention than money. Lillie had seen the sales of hats and shoes named after her flourish while debt-collectors carried away her furniture. Jordan received little for her fame beyond party invitations and her film fee, and it was some time before she began to perceive that others, less involved in punk, were making more money out of it. She began to ask for model fees for photographic sessions and money from those who photographed her on the street. 'It was very flattering, but cheques are also flattering,' as another street-fashion leader, this time in Manhattan, commented in an interview for British *Harpers & Queen* in September 1981. Colette, who was looking like a giant doll in Victorian rags and safety-pins while Jordan wore war-paint and black leather with zips, did not merely change her make-up and clothes for each change of image: she gave herself an entirely new name and personality. After ten years of Colette, whose style (fake flowers and pink mirrors) was, like her phrasing, faintly reminiscent of that other fashion heroine of the 1970s, Miss Piggy, Colette held a mock burial of herself and returned to the world as Justine, romantically dressed in satin and silk.

Her solution to the traditional difficulty of how to earn money from personal style and notoriety was to begin a company of her own, trademark 'Deadly Feminine', making clothes. Jordan's was to take her theatrical dressing not, like Lillie, to the world of the theatre, but to the world of pop music, where she made money and occasional appearances with Adam and the Ants. Personal publicity is a goose which, if treated correctly, may be persuaded to lay golden eggs.

But a woman may of course make fashions in her own circle without ever making her name. She may even see ripples of her influence spread outside it. In the period of fantasy dressing which followed punk, and which magazines and papers dubbed 'The New Romantic', there was no girl picked out by the press as a prototype, though she existed and was discovered by some. The New Romantics were less shocking and so less newsworthy than the punks. They were also less seen, because their dress was worn chiefly in night-clubs and discos rather than on the street. Julia starred in no film and was not asked her opinions on dress, art and society by the teenage magazines, though she modelled anonymously in a few. Lookalikes of her, however, could be seen in the favourite clubs of the young at the end of the 1970s. Far from rich, these

169

77   One of the first of the New Romantics, as the press termed them, Julia was a friend of
Steve Strange and dressed to her own ideas of chic on a tiny income. Seen in the height of
the New Romantic phase in the late '70s struggling on and off buses in a skirt which
hobbled her at the knee, high heels and a beehive hair-do, she was as closely imitated in
her social circles of night-clubs and discos as ever Georgiana, Lady Dudley was in hers. By
1982 Julia had moved on to a simpler style of dress but kept the tangled hair – product of
years of back-combing – and very defined make-up. Friends irritated her by expressing
nostalgia for her past looks. A girl with considerable natural style, she is photographed
here in what must be one of the most *Vogue*-like council-flat bedrooms in Britain.

escapists enjoyed the new craze for the dressing-up box. Small, white-
faced girls, with back-combed dark hair massed about their faces,
might be seen in Billy's Club, or eating out in cafés and wine bars,
dressed in little dark suits, tight round the knees, outlining their
curves, and with thickly applied dark red lipstick, or dripping with
black lace like tiny elegant spiders. Copies of some of the phases Julia
went through lingered, as did some of Jordan's make-ups, for years
after their popularisers had abandoned them.

Women of her kind, who influence the dress of others in their
restricted social circle, exist everywhere, recorded or unrecorded,
throughout the last hundred years. The influence operated in Julia's
case in the same way as that of famous Society leaders, like Georgiana
Dudley in the London of the 1870s. There was a Society round at which

to show off clothes, attended by a core of the same people to influence by degrees; an element of exclusivity and a small amount of publicity to stimulate interest and competition.

The Society round for the New Romantics was provided by regular nights at the same clubs and wine bars. Julia's friend, Steve Strange, provided the element of exclusivity on the same principle as Studio 54 in New York: by sitting at the door of Billy's Club and vetting those who wished to be admitted to it. Wealth and background were not factors. The New Romantics were chiefly teenagers and, if not unemployed, hardly rich. Julia herself came from Palmers Green and worked briefly as a hairdresser before she became a shop assistant. She sallied out, superbly dressed, from squats. Eventually publicity came, and photographers.

Julia's position as a fashion leader in this setting stemmed partly from natural beauty and partly from natural talent: she had a good eye for colour and detail. Half-Hungarian and half-English, she had been gifted with a milky skin, very dark eyes and hair, and supremely photogenic features. Had she been three inches taller than her five feet five inches, she could easily have earned her living as a model. Instead, she styled her own clothes according to her image. Indulging the typical shy, adolescent urge to act a part, she lived in a trance of dressing: choosing the kind of over-sophisticated clothes of a little girl playing at her mother's dressing table. It was the look of the 1950s: high heels, tight skirts, cinched leather jacket, shocking pink, figure-hugging dresses with split skirts, hair bouffant and back-combed, or folded into a French pleat. With it all went make-up thickly but carefully applied: deep lipstick, pale foundation, all chosen to match her clothes exactly. Handbags, shoes and gloves were chosen to co-ordinate with a precision which had not been urged by the fashion magazines for around fifteen years, and was not to become fashionable again until high fashion caught up with Julia's instincts about three years after she had dropped her high glamour style.

Like Jordan, she began to work as an assistant in the shop which sold the look: in her case, PX in Covent Garden. There and in night-clubs she received the many tributes, some new and some traditional, which the late twentieth century pays to its beauties. Fashion students asked to be able to photograph her for their projects; fashion photographers asked her to model for photo sessions; Luciana Martinez asked her to model for a portrait of her as Venus; her beauty was enshrined in video and her old style of dressing – she moved on to Victorian taffetas after her 1950s phase – was spoken of with depressing nostalgia by friends who clearly considered that her best, by twenty, already lay behind her.

Adventurousness and imagination marked the best of street dressing, and Ottoline Morrell might have enjoyed the New Romantics. It was in sharp contrast to the high fashion craze for standardised dressing at the beginning of the 1970s, when women of means could be seen sporting initials other than their own on their handbags, luggage, dresses, jeans and tops. Designers' signatures were flaunted to prove to onlookers that the wearers possessed money and taste. But it was someone else's taste, not theirs. The art of dress, and not the art of dressing, had been recognised: dresses were not only signed like paintings, they were studied, and the history of costume chronicled. The highest hopes of Mrs Haweis and Oscar Wilde for the recognition of dress as a subject for academic research had been realised, and it was possible to take degrees in the history as well as the design of dress. But the woman who wore clothes well at the centre of this artistic and creative endeavour remained uncredited.

The old prejudice that a deep interest in dressing indicated shallowness of mind was reinforced by the arguments of the feminist movement in the mid-1960s. Believing that feminine-looking clothes were an outward indication of subservience, the more extreme of them might be seen in the subservient dress of the working class man instead, short hair and boiler suit.

Germaine Greer more logically preferred to turn feminine clothes to aggressive purpose, saying that she wore very high heels in order to look down on men, but she too avoided high fashion. Her rather untidy, ethnic-looking dresses in the early 1970s were fairly typical of the compromise adopted by progressive young middle-class women who demonstrated their high-mindedness in unchanging flowing garments from Indian shops or cheap cotton smocks from Laura Ashley. Hampstead Woman was as earnest and sloppily dressed, as devoted to white walls and blue and white or pottery, as her Graeco-South Kensington predecessor, though she was concerned not with the romance of art but that of social justice. The philosophy of her dressing appeared to be that it was acceptable to dress in a feminine way so long as the clothes were comfortable, cheap and preferably made in a poor country.

The argument that feminism and fashion might not be mutually exclusive was made at last – led by Janet Radcliffe Richards in *The*

78 The early '70s, and a revival of a loose, romantic version of the aesthetic mode. Germaine Greer, sprawled on the floor, is eagerly read amongst the terra-cotta pots and Indian dresses of Hampstead.

Sceptical Feminist in 1980. Not only did she argue that the choice to dress to attract a man or please herself was part of a woman's legitimate freedoms, she bravely suggested that it might be one of woman's arts. 'Feminists are always going on about woman's culture. . . . Very few feminists, however, ever seem to get round to saying what woman's culture is. But surely one of the clearest areas (even though not necessarily the most important) is that of women's dress and personal adornment.'

However shocking to the boiler-suited, this theory comes as no surprise to women who, like Dame Freya Stark, discovered long ago by experiment that it was not necessary to look like a man or even a female peasant in order to demonstrate equality of mind. Dame Freya, who

173

79 Not in the least ashamed of her deep interest in fashion, Dame Freya Stark, explorer and Arabic scholar, cheerfully explained that she spent happy hours on her travels into the unknown chatting to the women she met about clothes. Her own clothes include a collection of Turkish and Arabic costume and an old lace bonnet, which she frequently wears at home: no liberated jeans for her, not even on horseback.

lists her interests in *Who's Who* as 'travel, mountaineering and embroidery', retained a passion for fine frocks and Paris modes throughout her career as an explorer and writer, and carried her white embroidery work with her on her journey in 1932 to discover Lamisiar, one of the last strongholds of the Assassins. Assuming that an interest in dress was an inalienable characteristic of the female – 'Must go back to Eve, don't you think,' she told John Julius Norwich in an interview – she collected Arabic dress as well as learning the language, and found it an endlessly interesting source of conversation with the women she met on her travels. Not only did she not despise her unliberated sisters in their harems, she counted on the chauvinism of men as an asset,

174

saying on her return from Luristan, 'I used to walk ahead of my miserable guide, because even a bandit would stop to ask questions before shooting when he saw a European woman strolling on alone, hatless.'

With a first female British Prime Minister in office, whose worst enemies never accused of frivolity but who cared enough about her appearance to take her heated rollers with her to keep her curls in place on her post-war visit to the Falkland Islands, it was difficult at the beginning of the 1980s for anyone to argue that a feminine appearance implied feather-headedness. Yet despite the new respectability of fashionable dressing it was not a writer or a politician who demonstrated in 1981 that there was an unimpaired demand for a female fashion leader. Lady Diana Spencer, as future Princess of Wales, represented a more traditional kind of success: with not a single 'O' level to her name, she was engaged to perhaps the most eligible bachelor in the world. Like Princess Alexandra a hundred years earlier, she rested on a reputation for virtue and looks, and her putative virginity was discussed by the press with as much enthusiasm as her dress sense. Her interests and ambitions were identical with those of the Dickensian heroine in that she was chiefly interested in children and her own marriage and she dressed without shame for her fiancé – 'Wonderful for you' was what lip-readers claimed that she replied to Prince Charles's compliment when she arrived at the end of St Paul's aisle on her wedding day.

Like Alexandra, she displayed the natural ease in dress of a girl who had been brought up in the circles in which she was marrying, for she was as used to the life of the great country estate as the town house. Her dress sense appeared as instinctive – if not, at first, quite as neat and tidy – as that of her predecessor, and she too had obviously absorbed much of it from a stylish mother. Mrs Shand-Kydd could be seen in the same pearl chokers, the same ruffled collars and romantic style as her daughter, and though Lady Jane Fellowes did not, like Dagmar, appear in identical dresses to those of her sister, she did appear at her wedding in white boater, Peter Pan white collar, red dress and pearl choker so close to Diana's usual look that it was clear that Diana's was a Spencer family style.

This time, when the engagement was announced on 24 February 1981, there was no shortage of details of the future bride's appearance for the female readership of magazines and newspapers. Every outfit she had appeared in for months before was scrutinised by fashion editors looking for details out of which to make copy, but as before it was the hair-style, short, highlighted and side-parted, which was the most identifiable and imitable characteristic. There were soon other strong features of what was incorrectly but inevitably dubbed the 'Princess Di' look to copy. Even those of the old, rigorous school of grooming, like Margaret, Duchess of Argyll, were impressed by the professionalism and speed with which she developed her own style. It was a make-over conducted in public, with each stage (and each mistake) recorded by photographs.

Her looks changed. Like Alexandra, and in response to the identical pressures of a busier life and the stress of public attention, she lost weight quickly before the wedding. The result, again as in Alexandra's case, was to make her face more photogenic as it lost its slight adolescent chubbiness. Make-up artists transformed her face for photographic sessions and public appearances. In her early engagement pictures she wears her blusher too high and too strong, and too harsh and dark an eye-liner. There was a gradual progression to a softer, subtler, more porcelain make-up.

Her clothes changed. All the mistakes of her early appearances – the see-through skirts, the uneven hems, the ill-fitting collars, the insecure low bodice on a black evening dress worn at Covent Garden, the hurriedly changed hem-length on the blue suit of her engagement pictures – were more clearly revealed by photographs than by any full-length mirror. Diana's post-engagement clothes were chosen with the help of professional expertise, and she had developed a far closer 'special relationship' with *Vogue* than that enjoyed by any previous royal bride, including Princess Marina and Mrs Simpson. It was not long kept a secret that *Vogue* editors were making initial selections of clothes for her, from which she was able to make her own choice without the designers even being aware that their garments had been under review. Unlike previous Princesses, who had kept to a small, safe collection of discreet dressmakers, Diana was able to range through the whole breadth of the British fashion trade and keep in constant touch with new names and fresh ideas. But despite the partnership she kept a distinctively personal style and did not simply reflect the looks which were shown in the pages of *Vogue*. Nor, because of the multitude of different labels she bought, was she associated with the creations of any particular designer, as Marina had been with Molyneux.

The constituents of the 'Princess Di' style were a romantic period flavour, ruffles and rich fabrics. In the post-austerity 1950s, Princess

80   A full circle of more than a century brings another new Princess of Wales, and another royal wedding at which the bride is tirelessly compared to a fairy princess and seems to dress for the part. A portrait by Sue Ryder of the Princess of Wales in her wedding dress, commissioned by Prince Charles, who clearly approves of the image.

Marina had been the first member of the royal family to appear for public engagements in cottons, and among the first to buy from Marks and Spencer. Diana, by contrast, at a time when the news was of firms closing and unemployment rising, appeared in rich velvets and silks by day and generally set them off with a few rows of pearls. Her dressing was escapist in style as well as material; she wore tricorne hats, sometimes with principal boy feathers in them, and even in the sailor collars rarely fashionable in 1981, she looked neither naughty nor nautical, but like a Victorian child. It was good-girl dressing – demure, soft, clinging or sexy. There were little-girl Peter Pan collars, flat shoes and wide sashes, and even the low necklines she affected in the evening were counterbalanced by sentimental frills and her ingenuous face. In her wedding dress, in particular, she could be seen to be playing the part of a story-book princess (though it was not designed especially for her – a slightly simpler version appeared in *Vogue* the June immediately before her wedding). With its great puffed sleeves, lacy frills and tiny waist, it was pure Cinderella, with a glass coach to match.

There were other signs that she was deliberately dressing for the camera and her rôles – more so, perhaps because she was new to the stage, than the women born into the royal family. Her small, tilted hats, white collars and chokers all framed her face and drew attention to it, making for excellent close-up photographs. Like Alexandra again, she was seen to dress for national sympathies: where Alexandra had worn shamrocks and Irish poplin for her visit to Ireland, Diana was seen in Wales in red and green, and at the Braemar Games in Scotland, twice running, clad head to foot in tartan.

She did not wear high fashion. Diana's clothes were no guide to what was happening on the catwalks of Paris, and even less so when, after the birth of her son in 1982, with lady-like thrift she brought out and wore again the wardrobe she had bought for herself the previous year.

As a result, she was not an influence on those who were keenly interested in fashionable clothes, who found that Diana's look lacked sophistication. Her influence operated most strongly amongst her own peer group – Collingwoods, family jewellers to many landed titles, reported in 1981 that heirloom chokers were being taken out of the safes again – and amongst those in the provinces at some distance from fashion trends, where Diana's appearance on the television news and in magazines brought them the news of fashionable items of dress, which were already well established amongst upper-middle-class girls in

London's Sloane Street, faster than it would usually have reached them. The flat or very low-heeled plain shoes, for example, in which Diana was photographed before her engagement, had been seen on London streets for some time. But with the influence of her example they were promptly identified outside fashion centres as 'Lady Di shoes'. Her photographs explained what clothes the shoes were worn with, and what age group wore them, as a shoe display could not. And they had an advantage over fashion magazine photographs in that they induced all the family to recognise them as an acceptable fashion trend. It was obvious to the most conservative mother or recalcitrant boy-friend that what Lady Diana wore was safe: she was not the kind of girl who appeared in potentially embarrassing clothes. She would not be seen in a ra-ra skirt.

She was, indeed, chiefly seen in formal clothes, the equivalent of the 'morning dress' of the previous century. Although, especially for minor appointments, she did not always appear in a hat, she was nonetheless usually seen in the kind of clothes, with handbag, gloves and shoes, worn by few of her mother-in-law's subjects of her age except at weddings. It was therefore at formal occasions that her style might be expected to have the most impact, and not on the street: there were few Diana lookalikes to be seen there.

Predictably, provincial hat shops changed stock from wide-brimmed mushrooms to tiny tricornes and small velvet pillboxes with veils. A chagrined reader wrote on 21 November 1982 to the *Daily Mail*, to complain that his 38-year-old wife had attempted the Princess Diana look for Ascot but been accused of imitating Nancy Reagan instead. Weddings, even more formal, where traditions in everything from dresses to music are set every quarter-century or so by a big royal event, showed the influence of the Princess of Wales's at every level. The direct copies of Diana's dress did not sell in great numbers, but dresses which incorporated the crinoline skirts and ruffles were suddenly more popular than the Edwardian high-necked, tight-skirted styles which had been selling well before 1981. Kate Greenaway bridesmaids, long popular in the Home Counties, made their appearance in London's East End.

Like Alexandra, Diana brought glamour to the royal family group – the present Queen, while hardly in widow's weeds, appears very little keener on fashion than Victoria was. And that the desire of women for romance and escapism had not died with more equal opportunities and education was demonstrated by the popularity of the frothy novels written by her step-grandmother, Barbara Cartland. Ann Edwards, writing in the *Sunday Express* on 31 October 1982 in Cartland-like terms, attributed some of the interest to the general contrasting misery of world and national news: 'Just to see her standing there in an exquisite emerald-green taffeta dress with emeralds round her throat, blonde hair burnished, looking at us with those huge blue eyes and a half-smile on her lips – that glimpse of the Princess of Wales attending a concert was a shaft of sheer delight piercing a gloomy week.'

But it is more than a reader demand for escapism which motivates fashion editors of newspapers to scrutinise each outfit of Diana's many appearances for possible fashion stories. A fashion leader interests more than a model simply because she exists in a real world, however privileged. Diana, despite her charming smile, is not, with her large, crooked nose and strong-boned face, as lovely as many a professional clothes-peg. But her stylishly put together and worn clothes have more significance than those on a catwalk because they reflect her personality and her life and are selected for particular occasions. The designer's fantasies have had to be restrained by Diana's needs. The Princess who is rumoured to have crushed one chattering, over-enthusiastic designer with the words, 'Back to your basket', demonstrates that the designer's rôle, as that of Worth to Eugénie, is co-conspirator and not dictator. Faces, to paraphrase Edith Sitwell, are being worn again.

Bibliography

Adams, Samuel & Sarah, *The Complete Servant*, 1825.

Adburgham, Alison, *Liberty's – A biography of a Shop*, 1975.

Adburgham, Alison, *A Punch History of Manners and Modes*, 1961.

Anon, *The Art of Dressing Well and The Laws of Good Society*, 1875.

Anon, *How to Dress on £15 a Year as a Lady*, 1873.

Argyll, Margaret, Duchess of, *Forget Not*, 1975.

Asquith, Lady Cynthia, *Diaries, 1915–18*, 1968.

Asquith, Lady Cynthia, *Remember and Be Glad*, 1952.

Baines, Barbara, *Fashion Revivals from the Elizabethan Age to the Present Day*.

Balsan, C. V., *The Glitter and the Gold*, 1953.

Battiscombe, Georgina, *Queen Alexandra*, 1966.

Beaton, Cecil, *Diaries. The Wandering Years: 1922–39*, 1961.
   The Years Between: 1939–44, 1965.
   The Happy Years: 1944–48, 1972.
   The Strenuous Years: 1948–55, 1973.
   The Restless Years: 1955–63, 1976.
   The Parting Years: 1963–74, 1978.

Beaton, Cecil, *The Glass of Fashion*, 1954.

Bernhardt, Sarah, *My Double Life*, 1917.

Blunden, Margaret, *The Countess of Warwick*, 1967.

Booth, Michael R., *Victorian Spectacular Theatre, 1850 to 1910*, 1981.

Bradley, Ian, *William Morris and His World*, 1978.

Buck, Anne, *Dress in Eighteenth-Century England*, 1979.

Campbell, Mrs Patrick, *My Life and Some Letters*, 1922.

Chase, E. W., *Always in Vogue*, 1954.

Chisholm, Anne, *Nancy Cunard*, 1979.

Churchill, Peregrine, and Mitchell, Julian, *Jennie, Lady Randolph Churchill*, 1974.

Collier, Constance, *Harlequinade*, 1929.

Comyns Carr, Mrs J., *Reminiscences*, 1926.

Cooper, Lady Diana, *The Rainbow Comes and Goes*, 1958.

Cooper, Gladys, *Gladys Cooper*, 1931.

Cornwallis-West, G. F. M., *Edwardian Hey-Days*, 1930.

Cornwallis-West, Mrs George, *The Reminiscences of Lady Randolph Churchill*, 1908.

Dobbs, Brian and Judy, *Dante Gabriel Rossetti, An Alien Victorian*, 1977.

Duff, David, *Alexandra, Princess and Queen*, 1980.

Easton, Malcolm, and Holroyd, Michael, *The Art of Augustus John*, 1974.

Easton, Malcolm, 'There Goes an Augustus John', *Costume* 8, 1974.

Fielding, Daphne, *Emerald and Nancy*, 1968.

Garland, Madge, *The Changing Face of Beauty*, 1957.

Garrett, Richard, *Mrs Simpson*, 1979.
Gernsheim, Alison, *Fashion and Reality, 1840–1914*, 1963.
Gernsheim, H. and L., *Edward VII and Queen Alexandra*, 1962.
Glendinning, Victoria, *Edith Sitwell*, 1981.
Glynn, Prudence, *In Fashion*, 1978.
Halls, Zillah, *Coronation Costume, 1685–1953*, 1973.
Harrison, Rosina, *Rose – My Life in Service*, 1975.
Hartnell, Norman, *Silver and Gold*, 1955.
Haweis, H. R., *The Art of Dress*, 1879.
Holroyd, Michael, *Augustus John – The Years of Innocence*, 1974.
Holroyd, Michael, *Augustus John, The Years of Experience*, 1975.
Howe, Bea, *Arbiter of Elegance*, 1967.
Howell, Georgina, *In Vogue*, 1975.
Hummell, Cecile, 'Conversation At Castle Howard', *Costume* 3, 1969.
John, Augustus, *Chiaroscuro*, 1954.
John, Romilly, *The Seventh Child*, 1975.
Julian, Philippe, *Oscar Wilde*, 1969.
Lang, Theo, *My Darling Daisy*, 1966.
Langtry, Lillie, *The Days I Knew*, 1925.
Lawrence, Gertrude, *A Star Danced*, 1945.
Lynam, Ruth, *Paris Fashion*, 1966.
Madol, Roger, *The Private Life of Queen Alexandra*, 1940.
Manvell, Roger, *Ellen Terry*, 1968.
Masson, Madeleine, *Edwina, Countess Mountbatten of Burma*, 1958.
McMullen, Roy, *Victorian Outsider*, 1974.
McVay, Gordon, *Isadora and Esenin*, 1980.
Moore, Doris Langley, *The Woman in Fashion*, 1947.
Morley, Sheridan, *Gladys Cooper*, 1979.
Marly, Diana de, *Worth, Father of Haute Couture*, 1980.
Morrell, Lady Ottoline (ed. Robert Gathorne-Hardy), *Early Memoirs of Lady Ottoline Morrell*, 1964.
Morris, Margaret, *My Life in Movement*, 1969.
Mosley, Diana, *The Duchess of Windsor*, 1980.
Nicholson, Nigel, *Mary Curzon*, 1977.
Paget, W., *Embassies of Other Days*, 1923.
Paget, W., *Scenes and Memories*, 1912.
Ponsonby, Sir Frederick, *Recollections of Three Reigns*, 1951.
Robertson, W. Graham, *Time Was*, 1951.
Rose, André, *The Pre-Raphaelites*, 1977.
Richardson, Joanna, *Sarah Bernhardt and Her World*, 1977.
Salter, Elizabeth, *Edith Sitwell*, 1979.
Saunders, E., *The Age of Worth*, 1954.
Shonfield, Zuzanna, 'Miss Marshall and the Cimabue Browns'. *Costume* 13, 1979.
Simon-Sykes, Christopher, *Country House Camera*, 1980.
Sitwell, Edith, *Taken Care Of*, 1965.
Stuart, Denis, *Dear Duchess*, 1982.
Swain, Margaret, 'Mrs Newbery's Dress'. *Costume* 12, 1978.

Terry, Ellen, *Story of My Life*, 1908.
Tinling, Ted, *Love and Faults*, 1979.
Tree, Viola, *Castles in the Air*, 1925.
Vanderbilt, Gloria, and Furness, Lady Thelma, *Double Exposure*, 1959.
Walkley, Christina, and Foster, Vanda, *Crinolines and Crimping Irons*, 1979.
Warwick, Frances, Countess of, *Life's Ebb and Flow*, 1929.
West, J. B., *Upstairs at the White House*, 1974.
Westminster, Loelia, Duchess of, *Grace and Favour*, 1961.
Windsor, Duke of, *A King's Story*, 1951.

Index

advertisement 44–6, 155–6
Alexandra, Queen (Princess Alexandra) 1, 4–27, 31, 38, 45, 55, 59, 62, 65, 69, 71, 72, 79, 91–2, 94, 121, 135, 139, 163, 175–8
Anderson, Mary 67
Argyll, Margaret Duchess of (Margaret Whigham) 139, 142–5, 150, 152, 154–6
Ashley, Lady (Sylvia Hawkes) 136
Asquith, Lady Cynthia 48, 101, 121, 126
Asquith, Margot 125
Astor, Lady (Bronwen Pugh) 158
Avery, Claire 103

Balenciaga 152, 165
Balmain 158
Beaton, Sir Cecil 2, 47, 113, 120, 129, 139, 150, 152
Beere, Mrs Bernard 67
Beeton, Mrs 25, 58
Bernhardt, Sarah 5, 42, 43, 44, 48, 52–4, 56, 62–3, 65, 67, 70, 72–3
Blossier, Morin 92
Boughton, Alice 103
Bridgman, Lady Lucy and Lady Charlotte 11
Burne-Jones, Georgiana 62

Campbell, Lady Colin 82
Campbell, Mrs Patrick (Stella) 47, 74, 82, 101
Casati Marchesa 120
Cassini Oleg 163
Castle, Mrs Vernon (Irene) 110–11, 115, 116
Chanel, Coco 138
Chase, Edna Woolman 103, 141
Choker 18, 178
Christian, Princess 8
Churchill, Lady Randolph (Jennie Jerome) 17, 22, 29, 36, 44, 82, 84
Cigarette cards 44
Clark, Ossie 165
Colette (Justine) 169
Collier, Constance 45–8, 101
Collingwoods 178
Comyns Carr, Mrs (Alice) 8, 18, 52, 55, 58, 63, 64, 70
Cooper, Gladys 45
Cooper, Lady Diana (Manners) 1, 70, 95, 112–16, 120, 121, 135, 151, 152, 155
Cornwallis West, Mary 32, 35, 84
Cox, Ka 100
Cranborne, Lady 145–6
Craig, Edie 102
Craven, Lady Mary 24
crinoline 11, 19–20, 51, 65, 179
Cunard, Maud 116

Cunard, Nancy 114–16, 128
Curzon, Lady (Mary Leiter) 88–94, 142
Cust, Mrs Henry 76

Dagmar, Princess 29
Déssès 152
Devonshire, Duchess of (also Duchess of Manchester) 2, 22–5, 71–2, 82
Devonshire, Duchess of's Ball, 1897 9, 73, 76, 92
Desborough, Lady 75
Dior 152, 162
Doucet 35
Dudley, Lady (Georgiana Moncrieffe) 13, 27, 29, 32, 38, 170
Dudley Ward, Mrs 138
Duncan, Isadora 70, 95, 104–7
Dunraven, Countess of 65

Elizabeth, Queen 119, 162
Elsie, Lily 95
d'Erlanger, Baroness 134
Eugenie, Empress 4, 9, 22, 36, 162

Fellowes, Daisy 147, 152, 156, 162
Fellowes, Lady Jane 175
Forbes, Lady Angela 80–6
Fortuny 67, 70
Furness, Thelma, Lady (Converse) 137–9, 150–2

Garbo, Greta 146
Garret-Anderson, Elizabeth 63
Gellibrand, Paula 128
Gibson, Charles Dana 88
Givenchy 152
Goalen, Barbara 158
Godwin, E. W. 51, 55, 56, 60, 167
Granby, Marchioness of – see Rutland, Duchess of
Greer, Germaine 172

Haberton, Lady 78
Hall, Jerry 27, 32, 160
Harlow, Jean 156–7
Hartnell 141, 144, 150, 162
Haweis, Mrs 2, 58–60, 62, 63, 65, 67, 112, 172
Head-scarves 100–1, 118, 119
Helvin, Marie 32
Hepburn, Audrey 162

Jagger, Bianca 165–6
Jap 161
Jerome, Clara 17, 24
Jerome, Jenny – see Churchill, Lady Randolph

Jerome, Leonie 17
Jewellery, importance for status 14, 43, 86, 154
    aesthetic 49, 59, 62–3, 72, 127
    fake 112, 118
John, Dorelia 2, 95–100, 104, 111–12, 116, 118–19
John, Ida 98–100
Jones, Louisa 17
Jordan 167–9
Journalism, coverage of leaders of fashion 3, 19,
    24–5, 43, 46–7, 58–9, 64–5, 79–80, 87–8,
    114, 118, 155
Julia 169–72

Kent, Princess Michael of 16
Kennedy, Jacqueline – *see* Onassis, Jacqueline

Langtry, Lillie 29–36, 38–45, 47, 49, 67, 84, 160
Lanvin 138
Lambert, Mrs 134
Laszlo, Dr Erno 146, 154
Lawrence, Gertrude 119, 121, 148–50, 154
Lee, Vernon 52n
Leigh, Vivien 150
Leiter, Mary – *see* Curzon, Lady
Lenglen, Suzanne 108–10
Lewis, Rosa 145, 146
Liberty 65
Lindsay, Violet – *see* Rutland, Duchess of
Lydig, Mrs Rita de Acosta 124
Lytton, Judith 133

Mainbocher 152
Make-up 24, 32–5, 53, 75, 113, 116, 118, 120, 124,
    126, 128, 142, 144, 158, 160
Manchester, Duchess of – *see* Devonshire,
    Duchess of
Manners, Marjorie 113
Manning, Maria 3
Margaret, Princess 119
Marina, Princess 60, 139, 151, 178
Marlborough, Consuelo, Duchess of 10, 13,
    84–8, 131
Martinez, Luciana 171
Maurier, George du 52, 65
Maynard, Daisy – *see* Warwick, Duchess of
Medici collar 18
Mendl, Lady 151
Metternich, Pauline von 20
Millar, Gertie 45
Millet, Maud 46
Molyneux 141, 150
Morrell, Lady Ottoline 24, 96, 101, 116, 120–6,
    130–4, 172
Morris, Jane 2, 29, 48, 52, 54, 56, 60, 62, 120
Morris, Margaret 107–8
Mountbatten, Lady Edwin Ashley 141, 142

Nettleship Mrs, 58, 98

Newbery, Mrs 62, 104
Nightingale, Florence 49
Nutter, Tommy 165

Olivia bonnet 58
Onassis, Jacqueline (Kennedy) 162–3
Ospovat 135

Paget, Lady (Walpurga) 8, 13, 26, 36, 69
Photography 2, 25, 27, 37, 43, 44, 79, 155, 156,
    158
Picture postcards 44
Plymouth, Countess of 74
Ponsonby, Loelia – *see* Duchess of Westminster

Reagan, Nancy 179
Reboux 138
Redfern 22, 36
Reville 46
Rhodes, Zandra 165
Richards, Janet Redcliffe 172–3
Rosenberg, Sonia 138
Rosse, Lady 154
Rutland, Duchess of (Marchioness of Granby,
    Violet Lindsay) 5, 29, 54, 72–6, 86, 113
Ryan, Elizabeth 108

St Laurent 162, 165
Sarony, Napoleon 44
Schiaparelli 152, 155
Scone, Lady 155
Sebright, Lady 30, 32
Shand-Kydd, Mrs 175
Shrimpton, Jean 158
Siddal, Elizabeth 29
Simpson, Mrs – *see* Windsor, Duchess of
Sitwell, Edith 120–9, 134, 158
smocking 60, 102–4
Snow, Mrs Carmel 119
Souls 71–6, 83, 86, 89
Spencer, Lady Diana – *see* Wales, Princess of
Stanhope, Lady Hester 133
Stark, Dame Freya 173–5
Stratton 36
Sun bonnets 101
suntans 95, 96, 100–1, 107, 115, 118–19
Sutherland, Millicent, Duchess of 15, 75

tailormades 18–22
tea gowns 67–70
Terry, Ellen 2, 8, 29, 48–52, 54–8, 60–3, 65–7,
    69–72, 75, 102, 105, 110
Thatcher, Mrs Margaret 175
Thyssen, Baroness von (Fiona Campbell Walter)
    158
Tree, Iris 112–16, 128, 135
Tree, Lady (Maud) 112, 115
Tree, Viola 112–15

trousers 43, 63, 78, 103, 116, 141
Tweedsmuir, Susan, Lady 95
Twiggy 158

Vanderbilt, Gloria (Converse) 137, 138
Victoria, Queen 4, 5, 8, 11, 23, 94
Victoria, Princess Royal 4, 5
Vionet 138
Vogue 88, 102, 103, 110, 112, 113, 119, 136, 154, 156, 162, 176
Vreeland, Diana 121

Wales, Princess of (Alexandra) – *see* Alexandra, Queen
Wales, Princess of (Lady Diana Spencer) 1, 25, 175–80
Warwick, Daisy Countess of (Maynard) 29–31, 38, 76–86, 95

Westminster, Loelia Duchess of (Ponsonby) 142, 148
Westwood, Vivienne 167–8
Wheeler, Mrs 32
Whigham, Margaret – *see* Argyll, Margaret Duchess of
Wilde, Constance 56
Wilde, Oscar 2, 31, 32, 43, 56, 59, 62, 82, 84, 85, 172
Wilding, Dorothy 155–6
Wilton, Lady 36
Wilkinson, Miss Annie 16
Windsor, Duchess of 2, 146–52, 155–6, 165
Woolf, Virginia 100, 124, 127, 128
Worth, Charles 4, 94
Worth, Jean 13, 36, 86

Yuki 70